COMMUNICATION AND DEVELOPMENT
The Challenge of the Twenty-first Century

By the Same Author

Communication Planning for Socio-Economic Development, (edited alongwith Ranjit Singh).

Media and Development, Themes in Communication and Extension, (edited alongwith M. R. Dua).

Third Revolution in Indian Perspective—Contemporary Issues and Themes in Communication

Rural Press—Problems and Prospects, (edited alongwith Rajeshwar Dyal).

Media Policy and Nation Building—Select Issues and Themes, (with Vir Bala Aggarwal).

National Media Policy, (edited alongwith Rajeshwar Dyal).

Media and Market Forces—Challenges and Opportunities (edited alongwith Rajeshwar Dyal).

Communication Technology, Media Policy and National Development

---

About the Author

V. S. Gupta, a senior media academic, is presently a Professor at Haryana Agricultural University. He was awarded UNDP fellowship for training in Europe and selected for the Journalist Fellowship Award for working in the areas of environment and development. He conceptualised and implemented as Course Director, the Post Graduate Diploma Course in Agricultural Journalism through Distance Education, and Refresher Course in Communication and Writing Skills in the University. As the Zonal/Country Representative for the Asia Media Information and Communication Centre (AMIC), Singapore, for a number of years, he organised numerous regional seminars and National Colloquium throughout the country, besides bringing out several publications. He is associated with a number of Universities as UGC Visiting Fellow, member of academic bodies and also with the Departments of Journalism and Mass Communication at the post-graduate and doctoral levels.

COMMUNICATION AND DEVELOPMENT
The Challenge of the Twenty-first Century

V. S. Gupta

CONCEPT PUBLISHING COMPANY, NEW DELHI-110 059

ISBN 81-7022-849-2

First Published 2000

Published and Printed by
Ashok Kumar Mittal
Concept Publishing Company
A/15-16, Commercial Block, Mohan Garden,
NEW DELHI - 110059 (India)

Phones : 5648039, 5649024
Fax : 091-11-5648053
Email : publishing@conceptpub.com

Preface

My engagement with the development and communication issues goes back to the early seventies when I joined Haryana Agricultural University in the Directorate of Extension Education and subsequently headed the Farm Information and Communication Service. The close interaction with the farmers, extension workers and publishing and communication professionals gave me the necessary insight into various aspects of rural development.

One of my first papers—Development Communication—An emerging concept—appeared in *Vidura* in 1979. Since then there has been a constant endeavour to understand and reflect on various aspects of development policy, its implementation, deficiencies, as well as how the media of communication could be harnessed to make development more meaningful and relevant to the intended beneficiaries.

When I sent a copy of my book, *Third Revolution in Indian Perspective—Contemporary Issues and Themes in Communication (1995)*, which had four chapters on different aspects of development to Mr. Gunter Lehrke, a senior media expert at Friedrich Ebert Stiftung, a German no profit organisation, he wrote : I thank you in particular for your pages on development communication since that term gives cause to many misapprehensions in different parts of the world. The media and communication development in India belongs to the most promising ones not only in the southern hemisphere but even in comparison to Europe. It is so rapid that your book will be outdated very soon. As far as India is concerned, I am very much impressed by the indepth discussion of the role of the media in the society among scholars, journalists and politicians, also reflected in your book. I sometimes wished that there would be a discussion of that quality in Germany too. In this part of the world the media is left more and more to the market and to commercial interests and people struggling for the survival of public service broadcasting, or—as I sometimes call it—"Broadcasting for public weal", get less and less. You can imagine that I sometimes incur the reproach of belonging to the last remaining socialists not completely realizing the blessing of market forces (*Bonn, 23 August 1995*).

The dilemma faced by Mr Lehrke is a matter of pervasive concern : Do we stand for deepening and refining our thinking about development, or we give in to the forces of the market, and concept of globalisation and corporatisation,

I feel optimistic that with the rethinking going on about models and paradigms of development, the 21st century will see less of poverty, deprivation and illiteracy.

26 January 2000 **V. S. Gupta**

Acknowledgements

I would like to gratefully acknowledge my deep gratitude to :

Asian Media Information and Communication Centre (AMIC), Singapore and its Secretary General, Mr. Vijay Menon; for his many acts of kindness to me over a long period of time;

Friedrich Ebert Stiftung, its resident representatives, Mr Rajeshwar Dyal, the Senior Media Advisor; and Mr Kabir Seth for continued association, good will and support;

The publisher, Mr Ashok Mittal for putting up with delays on my part;

My several colleagues and associates including Dr. Vir Bala Aggarwal and Sucharita S. Eashwar, Voices, Bangalore;

And above all a large cross-section of readership throughout the country, who have, by and large, been appreciative of my efforts all these years.

V. S. Gupta

Contents

List of Tables

1

Introduction and Overview

As the world enters the 21st Century, development issues—alleviation of poverty, eradication of illiteracy and ignorance, environmental protection, health and population concerns and preservation of human dignity and culture would continue to confront governments, civil society organisations, economic and social planners and institutions as major challenge. Each of these development issues is a challenging one; but during the latter half of the nineteenth century systematic thinking has gone into studying and analysing various aspects of these concerns. There has been rethinking all around as to why even after almost half a century of planning at the national and international levels, our accomplishments have not been commensurate with the efforts put in.

Development has been the dominant theme of the international discourse in the decades following the second world war. It has been a search rather than an achieved goal and the goal continues into the millennium and beyond.

Today development is one of the human rights and achieving development is no longer what the state may opt to "do". It is now the primary responsibility of the government to create national and international conditions favourable to the realization of right to development. The Declaration on Right to Development is particularly significant for its importance to developing countries.

Apart from the right to development, another basic and equally significant entitlement to human survival is right to communicate. Some governments, notably the United States, have included communication right as a basic right for their citizens. The Universal Declaration of Human Rights under Article 19 states : Everyone has the right to freedom of opinion and expression. This right includes freedom to hold opinions without interference and to seek, receive and impart information and ideas through any media and regardless of frontiers. As a result the right to information and communication is receiving greater attention in the contemporary affairs.

Development has become global "civil religion", during the past more than 40 years—a battle cry for all nations—rich or poor, strong or weak. It is a long and complex evolutionary process—more a process of social change rather than merely generation and accumulation of economic resources. Development thinking has evolved into a broad spectrum realization that it must move beyond economic growth to include important social goals—reduced poverty, improved quality of life, enhanced opportunities for better education and health, and more. Experience has also taught that sustainable progress towards these goals requires integrated implementation and must be firmly anchored in processes that are open, participatory and inclusive.

Development—in order to be impactive and durable—has to be sustainable. The *World Development Report* 1999/2000, *Entering the 21st Century* says : Sustainable development has many objectives. Raising per capita incomes is only one among many such objectives. Improving quality of life involves more specific goals : better health services and educational opportunities, greater participation in public life, a clean environment, intergenerational equity and more. Outcomes of policies based on consensual, participatory and transparent processes, are more easily sustained. Institutions of good governance that employ such processes are critical for development and should encompass partnership among all elements of civil society.

The development issue is characterised by its scale and magnitude. It is perceived more and more to be with broad masses of people—the development tide is turning more and more to favour the people—for instance now we have goals like *Education for All, Health for All.* However, the universalitic trend is riven by a development gap between advanced and poor countries. The development agenda is bypassing the poorer nations.

There has, however, been a refreshing rethinking and realisation that single-thrust industrialization has created deprivation and marginalization of children, women and the depressed poor. This rethinking is crystallised in the expression of regret on the part of Professor Tinbergen, who propounded the concept of GNP as a measure of progress. The use of GNP is steering the society with a wrong compass. GNP gives, imperfectly and somewhat deceptively, a measure of the aggregate value of national goods and services. It conceals the distribution of wealth and gives a deceptive picture of social health. Since the computation of GNP is not accompanied by a computation of Gross Destruction of Basic Resources (GDBR)—soil degradation, pollution of water and the atmosphere, depletion of mineral resources, the entry of toxic wastes in the food chain, and so on—it is a faulty indicator of economic health.

This work explores different aspects of development issues confronting the contemporary Indian society. The contribution that media of communication can make towards resolving these serious challenges—which for centuries have hindered the onward progress of the Indian society is also explored.

The book has been divided in two thematic sections. The first section comprises two chapters: Development Communication—Definitions and Concept, and the Indian Communication Landscape. The first chapter looks at various definitions and interpretations of the term development and its evolution now as a process of social change rather than merely generation and accumulation of material resources. An interesting reference is to the evolution of the World Bank's notion on the process of economic development and revisions and modifications of established doctrine of "growth-first-and-let-equality-come-later" and trickle down theories.

The World Development Reports and several international conferences on issues like environment, population and development have underscored the shift in emphasis and priorities by pointing out that people are the most valuable resources and puts man at the centre of development. The new development paradigm also stresses more investment in the social sector—such as health, education and nutrition. The chapter encapsulates the importance of communication in human life; for without communication no society can exist and no social structures would survive and flourish; and also discusses different perspectives of humanistic goals as well as multi faceted nature of development—economic, social, political and cultural aspects. The new development communication perspectives underline community orientation—community radio, community listening groups, voluntary action, etc. Equally important is participation as a part of communication process. In fact development, participation and communication form a part of a continuum.

The second chapter in the section takes an overview of the media landscape in the country and discusses a wide range of communication media, extending from inter-personal methods of communication to satellite broadcasting, from a two page broadsheet in a regional language to multi-edition daily printed through facsimile printing process, burgeoning television and cable TV system, and now the emerging multi-media and internet revolution in urban area. Interestingly even today, in spite of the vastly expanding media of mass communication, interpersonal communication through spoken word continues to enjoy predominant position particularly in rural areas. Similarly, traditional communication forms—folk theatre, folk tales, religious discourses have been used as means of disseminating information in the Indian villages. The mass media have made people aware of the unexpected wealth of folk and tribal music and exposed folk artists to the cultural diversity of the country.

Likewise, it has been pointed out that only when media channels could mix with interpersonal channels and with organisation in villages, development process will be effective.

Language press segment is playing a strategic role in print media, with single daily domination in several states enjoying a readership and circulation ranging from one-third or more to total circulation and readership. The language newspapers, closer as they are to the local communities, reflect the cultural and social traditions of the people they serve. Regarding the expansion of electronic media an interesting fact emerging from the district and mofussil towns of the country is that radio is still a widely used medium in the country. Since radio is the poor man's medium and is non-elitist, that is why it rarely figures in medium seminars, and therefore the skewed perception that it has become a museum fit tool to be stored in attic. As a tool for development communication reaching out to the people with relevant messages and usable information and to encourage peoples's participation in the 'Open Forum' which it eventually provides, community radio is an ideal medium. Several recent studies undertaken as a part of Post-Graduate Diploma Course in Agricultural Journalism on media-related issues, clearly prove that, contrary to popular impression about marginalisation of radio, it continues to serve the village community effectively through its farm broadcasts. Of the 18 research projects taken up by the participants of the 1999 batch, five pertained to radio. Studies on radio show that in the era of computer and information technology, the farmers still depend on radio for dissemination of farm news and technologies. From the number of radio sets available and in use by the farmers in rural areas and the frequency and variety of programmes related to agriculture and rural development, including programmes like Farm Radio School, it is apparent that radio still enjoys primary importance in disseminating messages of rural development. The policy makers and planners, in both the sectors—development as well as information and communication—need to re-order their priorities and densify radio broadcasting, in terms of number of radio stations, availability of cheap radio sets and larger budgetary allocation for staff recruitment and upgradation of their knowledge and skills. The continued step motherly treatment meted out to radio broadcasting signifies a particular mind set of policy planners which is conditioned more by glamour and hightech hype rather than the hard realities of human condition of the rural poor and the marginalised sections of the Indian society. The priorities have to be changed in favour of encouraging radio broadcasting. After all only 29 per cent of the population owes television sets and only 7 per cent of these have colour sets. That the Indian television has become primarily a medium for family entertainment and development programmes do not enjoy a large viewership has also been highlighted by a Doordarshan study. The study conducted by the Audience Research Unit of Doordarshan during January-March 1993, covering 420 villages from 15 states, observed that though Doordarshan entertainment programmes have a large viewership in villages, the development oriented programmes do not enjoy the same popularity. This study also collected information about the average number of persons watching a particular programme from one set, whereas nine viewers watched film-based programmes, only two opted for the programmes on agriculture.

The recent years have witnessed developmental growth in the media industry, particularly in electronic and satellite communication, and rapid advances in communication technology. Massive growth of television has been primarily due to operationalisation of INSAT satellite system in 1982, the live coverage of the gulf war by CNN in 1991; which led to the proliferation of transnational foreign satellite programmes. Another wave of looking at the television expansion in the country is the reach of Doordarshan in 1998 increased to 86 per cent of population as against 25 per cent in 1980; the number of programme production centres has gone up from 10 to 45 during the same period. The number of programmes produced by Doordarshan catering to the specific needs of languages and regions has also substantially increased; as also the number of TV households from 6.8 million in 1985 to 63.2 million cable and satellite households in the country.

In a case study 'TV Contents in Asia : More Waste or Substance', S. R. Joshi says : But the overall major thrust is one of entertainment of soap opera kind. Quite a few of the Indian language channels depend on the Indian feature film industry for providing this entertainment. This includes both showing of feature films as well as feature film based programmes like songs and dances, etc. The Training and Development Communication Channel (TDCC) of ISRO is using television for Training Panchayati Raj elected representatives; Aanganwadi workers, primary school teachers, mid-wives, etc. This network-TDCC is spreading out to several states and distance education agencies like Indira Gandhi National Open University (IGNOU), All India Management Association, NGO's like Self Employed Women Association (SEWA) and Ahmedabad Women's Action Group (AWAG). However, there is greater need to reorient TV programmes, also to make use of non-dominant forms of communication to respond to development needs of the target groups. Likewise the possibility of multi-media technology including internet to harness the requirements of development objectives has yet to be explored in the right earnest.

The second section of the book looks at specific issues—literacy, education and distance learning, rural development and poverty alleviation, health and population concerns and the challenges of human rights and environmental protection.

As the country moves towards higher level of economic and social development the contribution of education to nation building becomes crucial.

In developing countries the emphasis is on basic education including literacy. Since this is vital to their progress, it is not only an important input for economic growth but also a necessary element in participatory democracy. In developed countries, the infrastructure and systems to assume basic education are already in place.

Their focus is, therefore, on higher and continuing education. In both categories of countries, there is growing recognition about the critical role of education. In recent years, major international agencies, too have accorded priority to education—UNDP through its Human Development Reports and of late, World Bank, Trained manpower throughout the world and more so in societies, is becoming a precious resource. With the growing criticism of the centres of training and education, the universities in most of the countries are in the danger of becoming redundant and insignificant, as they cater to the privileged few. The recent trend towards free market economy has also made more and more countries realize the need for providing an easy access to affordable higher education to the masses.

The rapid obsolescence of knowledge requires individuals to make special efforts to stay-up-date. This means that one can collect, process and disseminate information very quickly. Television and radio satisfactorily meet this criterion. Also, learning has to be at the pace and knowledge level of the viewer. This implies the use of viewer controlled technologies so that the viewer may learn at a time convenient to him. Apart from other reasons, this clearly indicates that continuing education has necessarily to be based on distance learning modes. The need for earning while learning is another factor that is bound to make distance education the preferred form of the future.

One cannot enter the contemporary social and communication order if one is not literate, "An illiterate person has hundreds of enemies epidemics, hunger, disorder and humiliation", said the Soviet Government's statement on elimination of illiteracy makes one also victim of false information and false consciousness. Therefore, the key to progress is education which alone can uplift a society. Human Development Report 1995 lays great stress on women's education when it says that a year's schooling can increase a woman's future earnings by about 15 per cent. Hence, the role of education in nation building.

In this respect the efforts of the National Open School,

to bring basic education within the ambit of distant education system need to be stepped up further. The National Open School, in collaboration with the National Literacy Mission, hopes to reach out to 46 million neo-literates, who missed out on proper schooling in their childhood but wish to resume their education again. The women, who constitute 63 per cent of the neo-literates (having learnt to read and write but failed to sustain their learning after having dropped out from the school due to social and economic constraints), would be target group for this programme. The contemporary thinking is largely based on the realization that economics are built not merely through accumulation of physical capital, human resources and skills, but on a foundation of information, education and continuous process of learning.

The World Development Report 1998-99, Knowledge for Development says : KNOWLEDGE IS CRITICAL FOR DEVELOPMENT, because everything we do depends upon knowledge. Simply to live, we must transform the resources we have into the things we need, and that takes knowledge. And if we want to live better tomorrow than today, if we want to raise our living standards as a household or as country and preserve our common environment we must do more than simply transform more resources in ways that generate ever-higher returns of our efforts and investments. That too takes knowledge, and in ever greater proportion to our resources.

The need for developing countries to increase their capacity to use knowledge cannot be over stressed. It will be long time before literacy and education status in the country presents a satisfactory situation, what can still be taken up with certain amount of satisfaction is the belated realization that unless radical·changes are initiated in redesigning social policies, including those in basic education and elementary health care, the prospects of raising the general living standards of the population in the country would continue to be none too bright. The contemporary society is characterised by swift pace of change which affects our lives in diverse ways : rapid technological development, faster evolution and aggregation of knowledge rising aspirations of the people towards a more fulfilling quality of life, and increasing demand for qualified and trained manpower. Therefore, it is imperative that potential of communication technologies for educational purposes not in the restricted sense of structured formal academic system, but by way of opportunities for life long learning available throughout the life span of an individual be further strengthened.

In a nostalgic piece of writing, the doyen of Indian journalists and the Director of the Press Institute of India, Ajit Bhattacharjea says : Reporters with the *Statesman* in the fifties were obliged to make regular visits into the countryside to report on the state of harvest, pests, rainfall and other factors affecting rural life. Today agriculture is ignored by the national press except for occasional sponsored features. The journalists range of coverage is increasingly limited to the wired world of computer and telephone (The Problem, Media Trends, *Seminar*, October 1997).

The same is largely true of electronic media except for radio. The major TV programme on agriculture and rural development, *Krishi Darshan* continues to be uninspiring. Several research studies have established that this programme, which does not meet the felt needs of farmers, needs to be drastically reformated in its entirety. It needs to be examined as to why television has failed to put up programmes specific to the requirements of rural viewers, whereas the radio has richly contributed to the programmes of village uplift and rural development. Today a popular rice variety is known as "radio variety" because the variety was made popular through radio, on the other hand television has not been able to forge such relationship with the rural masses.

The situation is particularly reprehensible because rural development continues to be the *sine qua non* of the planned development in the country. The development efforts in the past have not fully taken into account social and community needs, cultural values and capabilities as key elements in rural development programmes. There is now belated realization that the needs of the people should be at the core of the development process which should be driven by social and environmental concerns rather than economic considerations alone.

In the subsequent Five Year Plans, the Planning Commission observed : What matters is not the precise increase in national product that is achieved in five or ten years, but whether we can assure, within a specified time frame, a measurable increase in the welfare of the millions of the poor. It is now accepted that rural development should mean not only an increase in the per capita GNP but greater equality in its composition. This would involve greater emphasis on social services like health, education, and welfare of the poor.

The communication perspective for rural development takes notes of summaries of research projects in agricultural information. The Course, introduced at the Haryana Agricultural University, in 1996 as a Distance Education programme for the faculty of agricultural universities and development workers of the states from all over the country, aims at imparting insights and skills in development communication. The Course has drawn its participants from Andaman and Nicobar to Tamil Nadu, Karnataka, Tripura and other states.

It would be relevant to mention the initiative taken by the Press Institute of India in taking up the publication of *Grassroots*, a monthly tabloid in English and Hindi. The *Grassroots* brings to its readers the news stories from Andhra villagers in search of drinking water, right to information campaign in Rajasthan and the success stories of NGOs. The August 1999 issue highlights the exploitation of Orissa tribals for bauxite (the adverse impact on the local population of alumina and bauxite mining projects located on tribal land in the Rayagada) and the November issue announces award for the best feature to Richard Mahapatra on villagers protecting forests in Orissa.

The chapter, Health, Population and Communication Strategy, underlines importance of the willing acceptance and participation of the people for the successful implementation of the health and population programmes, enhancing reproductive facilities for women—an aspect which had been generally ignored for years; and the effective contribution which the civil society organisations can make to this sector of nation building. The situation in the health and population sector continues to pose formidable challenge to the government and the policy planners in the country, also because public spending on health has been declining over the years. In terms of health infrastructure, countries like China and Sri Lanka are way ahead of India. The thorough going underactivity of the government in the health sector has been pointed out by Nobel laureate Amartya Sen who says : Among the different forms of interventions that can contribute to the provision of social security, the role of health care deserves forceful emphasis. Illness is, obviously enough, one of the most widespread causes of human deprivation and economic insecurity in India. It affects not only the actual patients and those who depend on them for their subsistence, but also other members of the society, in so far as the *threat* of disease arising from widespread morbidity reduces the quality of life.

After the International Conference on Population and Development (1994), the Government of India has made provision for the reproductive health needs of the women. The poor reproductive health situation in India and particularly that of the Indian women calls for a women-centred orientation including strategies to empower women in terms of control of economic resource, information and education, and enhancement of their rights.

It is now generally accepted that the target oriented, heavy handed approach, with an element of coercion created an adverse impact and a mind set which was not conducive to the successful implementation of the family planning programme. The programme instead of becoming a people's movement and people's concern, has become a preoccupation with the government alone. For the population welfare programme to succeed it is essential that attention be paid, at the same time to strengthen the movements for empowerment of women and female literacy. It is impossible to conceive the successful implementation of a vast national programme of family welfare without the cooperation of local bodies, particularly panchayati raj institutions, voluntary and non-governmental organisations. No government can build a society, whereas voluntary action can. The voluntary bodies have more freedom to articulate their point of view, raise consciousness, motivate and mobilise people.

In the ultimate analysis the challenge of increasing population explosion would be met only if it is understood in the proper perspective, particularly by the political leadership. It is essential that the leadership of all the political parties at the national and state level exhibit a firm commitment towards the success of family planning programme. The programme also needs to be linked with sustainable development, environment, empowerment of women and social and gender equity.

The incorporation of rights to development and communication, as a part of Human Rights Movement has once again underscored the importance of these two rights with which this work is essentially concerned. Promotion and protection of human rights in a plural society under a democratic framework requires sustained efforts of the government and non-governmental organizations at different levels. An independent judiciary and vigilant media are essential institutions to safeguard people's rights. The Human Rights are universally accepted; however, a successful mechanism to enforce them is yet to be developed. The United Nations and other international organizations; several well known non-governmental organizations including Amnesty International; in India the People's Union of Civil Liberties and the media; have been spearheading a movement to create greater awareness about these rights; yet much remains to be done in this vast undone area.

According to the former Chief Justice of India and presently chairperson of the National Human Rights Commission, Justice J. S. Verma, human rights are the *acknowledged index of civilisation in the international community*. Stressing the need to create people-friendly human rights culture, in a recent letter to the chairpersons of the existing eleven state human rights commissions,

Justice Verma regretted that there had not been any significant decline in genuine complaints of human rights violations and also pointed out lack of sensitivity on the part of prison staff to the basic human rights of the prisons. *Tribune*, 20 January 2000. Since the police and jail administration are considered as the agencies primarily responsible for the human rights violation in most of the cases constant efforts will have to be made in the direction of improving human rights conditions in these two departments.

The state of environment continues to pose a major challenge before the country in the 21st century. Despite several wake up calls, ecological movements in different parts of the country and judicial intervention, industrial and vehicular pollution continues to rise rapidly. A highly redeeming feature of the movement to protect the environment however has been the initiative taken by women, a number of social activists, individuals and institutes as also non-governmental organisations like Kerala Sastra Sahitya Parishad (KSSP). It would be relevant to refer to the contribution and role of KSSP to development issues like literacy campaigns. Silent Valley protection movement, and dissemination of scientific culture in Kerala and even beyond.

It would not be an exaggeration to say that KSSP is the most committed grassroot organisations in the third world which is as concerned about development as it is with environment. Its techno-economic assessment of the Silent Valley project remains by far the best multi-disciplinary document of its kind—and a lesson to environmentalists in Bombay and other cities with access to far greater funds than these teachers and scientists could ever hope to enjoy (Darryl D. Monte, Silent Valley, the Silence Returns, *Illustrated Weekly of India*, 15-21 April, 1984).

The several successful movements to protect environment in the country present a genuine effort on the part of individuals, groups and civil society organisations which Amartya Sen calls as *Public Action*. According to Sen : There are many failures particularly in the development of public educational facilities, health care provisions, social security arrangement, local democracy, environmental protection and so on ...... India's democratic institutes provide many potential bases of public action including not only the electoral process but also the news media, the legal system, village panchayats, etc.

It appears that the movement for environmental protection would make headway effectively only when it becomes a part of agenda of political parties on the pattern of the *Greens* in Europe, where by entering the political arena the parties are fighting elections on an ecological platform. At the same time it would also be important to stress that no steps for environmental protection will succeed unless our future plans are formulated keeping in view the broad consideration sustainable of development which is essentially concerned with intergenerational equity.

India—with its vast population of 1 billion people—with seventy per cent living in rural areas— severely need more such initiatives. Let it not be said of its planners, writers and communication experts that they showed no propensity to solve the problems such as alleviation of poverty, illiteracy and lack of guidance and sharing of development experience with other sections of society to make development an all-encompassing and participatory process.

2

Development Communication— Definitions and Concepts

The evolution of the term 'development' has had a fascinating history about itself. It has been open to large number of definitions, connotations and interpretations. The term has engaged and invited a multidisciplinary approach because of the vastness of the canvas it encompasses within its ambit.

In its broadest sense, 'development' tends to be an umbrella under which several phenomena—varying from human and spiritual development to economic and community development, as well as technological development have become related. Defining 'development' is not an easy task. It has been interpreted in various ways by sociologists, economists and development planners. They defined the term according to their own frame of reference. Modernisation, social change and enhancing quality of life are often used in one way or the other in explaining the term. In all cases development suggests some amount of improvement, self reliance, uplift and progress as also awareness and self-awareness to some extent.

Development has become the global 'civil religion' during the past more than 40 years—a battle cry for all nations rich or poor, strong or weak. It is a long and complex evolutionary process—more a process of social change rather than merely generation and accumulation of material resources.

Our understanding and perceptions about the process of development have undergone radical changes during the last 40 years. The earlier thinking about development during the sixties was dominated by Rostow's theory of economic growth. Researchers looked upon development as economic growth in stages without emphasizing the need for structural changes in society. and without indicating which sectors of the population in a developing country should receive the attention of planners and policy makers. The theory of economic growth, propounded by W. W. Rostow pointed out the following stages of economic growth :

1. the traditional and stagnant low per capita stage;
2. the transitional stage in which pre-conditions for growth are laid down;
3. the "take-off" stage marking the beginning of the process of economic growth; and
4. the industrialized, mass production and consumption stage, which makes for self-sustaining growth.

This approach emphasised capital accumulation, growth of labour force and the technological progress as the principal components of economic growth. It was assumed that economic growth in per capita Gross National Product would spread the benefits throughout the economy and eventually reach all groups. The theory failed to explain economic backwardness of many countries, particularly those who inherited it as a part of colonial legacy and it was not sufficiently sensitive to poverty. Rostow assumed that people in developing countries would respond rationally to economic incentives. The theory also assumed that once leading sectors of industry were advanced. their advantages would trickle down to the other sectors of economy.

The dominant thinking about development during this period was that, capital intensive technology imported from advanced countries, would lead to economic growth, industrialization and increase in per capita income—which by itself would lead to improvement in the living standards of the population. This paradigm of development was influenced by the western model—emphasis on industrialization—hydroelectric dams, huge steel mills and manufacturing industries. The development was essentially capital and technology intensive with agriculture receiving low priority. The planning for economic growth—which was synonym with development—was devised and executed by central governments. Development was quantified only in terms of aggregate or per capita basis. The thinking was encapsulated in terms of "growth-first-and-let-equality come later", and trickle down theories.

The opening years of the seventies saw a number of studies, new methods of analysis and new concepts which helped enhance understanding of development process, development policies and policies of development assistance. The causes which led to under-development of economies in the Third World countries were redefined. The western models of development assumed that main causes of under-development lay within the underdeveloped nation rather than any external factors responsible for it. Some of these were : traditional peasantry unresponsive to technological changes, fatalistic character of the population, land tenure system, etc.

In an illuminating essay on, World Bank's Concept of Development, J. H. Adler records the evolution of World Bank's notion on the process of economic development—how the concept of development process, has continuously changed, with new radical departures forcing revisions and modifications of some parts of what appeared to be firmly established doctrine. The period 1962-68, was that of, Revision of Convictions, during which agriculture and industry were identified as sectors deserving more attention; the announcement in 1963 that the Bank would be willing to finance educational projects constituted indeed a "new departure". According to Adler : The change resulted from the—obviously belated—recognition that under some conditions acceleration of the growth rate required not only an increased supply of capital, but also of other factors, especially skills. The Bank's willingness to provide financial support for education also reflected the previously mentioned view that development was inevitably slow; investment in education was accepted as yielding net returns with a high present value even if its full benefits could be expected only after a long gestation period.

The early and mid 1960s saw a change in World Bank's view and recognition of the complexity of development process. The period from 1968 onwards saw sharpness of break with earlier attitudes. Development was taken as a process of social change. It was being increasingly recognised that chances of attaining an orderly process of development were closely related to the effectiveness of measures *to distribute the gains of development equitably*; or atleast reasonably equitably among income groups, regions and sectors. This implies, for instance that in the formulation of a strategy for agricultural development the makers of development policy and providers of development finance must pay attention to the small and subsistence farmer and his participation in the development process.

One of the important conclusions regarding evolution of the World Bank's view on the process of economic development during some twenty years is : There is no short cut to development—neither via industrialization, nor via import substitution, infrastructure investment, or education. On the contrary; the only firm conclusion that emerges from twenty years of observation, analysis and action is that the path to development is far longer and much more arduous than it appeared to be when the conscious drive towards development, and development aid, began some twenty years ago.

Today the World Bank takes into consideration not only social change, but also includes cultural, ethical and spiritual issues to understand more intimately the development process. Unthinkable a few years ago, leading religious leaders from around the globe reached a landmark accord with the World Bank in 1998 to put moral and social values back into the financial grants balance sheets. So far the World Bank had ignored the importance of such values in development projects because it had focussed primarily on economic parameters.

Entering the 21st Century, World Development Report 1999/2000, released recently takes note of new directions in development thinking, outlook for comprehensive development and the shifting landscape at the dawn of the 21st century. The Report agrees that with nearly 1.5 billion people living on less than $ 1 a day and more than 2 billion on less than $ 2 a day, the task is indeed daunting.

After over 50 years of seeking to reduce poverty and disease and educate the poor, the World Bank admitted that many of its past policies were misguided and it needed help to succeed in the future.

The Report painted a bleak picture of a developing world which has fallen even further behind rich nations despite the efforts by the World Bank and others to make the world a better place to live.

It also said that in many ways the Bank had failed in its mission to improve conditions of poverty, disease and poor education in the developing world. Simple solutions—investments in physical and human capital, for instance, and unfettered markets—will not work in isolation, the report said, admitting its past focus had been misguided. Governments, the private sector, civil society and donor organisations need to work together in support of broad based development.

The conceptual frameworks for development of the past 50 years ... tended to focus too heavily on the search for a single key to development, the report noted. When a particular key failed to open the door to development in all times and places, it was set aside in search for a new one. Projects like building dams—something the World Bank was prolific in, during the 1950s and 1960s—can carry hidden costs and harm communities through population dislocation and other cultural and environmental problems. The Report says : Trickle-down economics—the practice of cutting taxes for the rich hoping it would benefit the poorer in society—does not work.

But whatever policies were used over the past 50 years, one thing is certain : poverty continues to rise. Today 1.5

billion people live on an income of less than $ 1 a day, up from 1.2 billion people in 1987. The report forecast the number living at that lowest of incomes would reach 1.9 billion by 2015.

The gap between the rich and the poor has also widened. Between 1970 and 1985 the average per capita income for the world's poorest countries dropped from 3.1 per cent of incomes in rich countries to just 1.9 per cent*.

The delegates of the developing nations at the United Nations Conference on Human Environment at Stockholm in 1972 attempted to look at the problems of under-development with a fresh perspective.

The work of two leading economists, E. F. Schumacher, who initiated a new philosophy of development with his book *Small is Beautiful*, and Andre Gunder Frank, who considered capitalism as the main cause of exploitation and inequality caused considerable rethinking about development.

The eminent communication scholar, Everett M. Rogers, has documented this process of rethinking about development in his book *Communication and Development—Critical Perspectives* (1976), as under :

> We summarize these newer conceptions of development by defining development as a widely participatory process of social change in a society, intended to bring about both social and material advancement (including greater equality, freedom, and other valued qualities) for the majority of the people through their gaining greater control over their environment (Rogers, 1975).

Thus, the concept of development has been expanded and made much more flexible, and at the same time more humanitarian, in its implications.

Rogers, at the same time, takes note of change in thinking as to the definition of development in the previous seven years. According to the earlier definition:

---

* Reuters Report in the *Times of India*, 20 September, 1999.

Development is a type of social change in which new ideas are introduced into a social system in order to produce higher per capita incomes and levels of living through more modern production methods and improved social organization (Rogers with Svenning, 1969). Rogers's approach to development articulated human concerns, as against economic concerns, and the emphasis shifted from GNP to distribution of fruits of development to all segments of society. The approach was participatory which underlined the importance of values such as equality and freedom. The approach was basically communication approach as compared with Rostow's authoritarian model of capitalism and industrialization.

Nothing highlights the rethinking on development as forcefully as the regret expressed by Professor Tinbergen, who propounded GNP as measure of progress. Tinbergen says : The use of GNP is steering the society with a wrong compass. GNP gives, imperfectly and somewhat deceptively, a measure of the aggregate value of national goods and services. It conceals the distribution of wealth and gives a deceptive picture of social health. Since the computation of GNP is not accompanied by a computation of Gross Destruction of Basic Resources (GDBR)—soil degradation, pollution of water and the atmosphere, depletion of mineral resources, the entry of toxic wastes in the food chain, and so on—it is a faulty indicator of economic health. Similarly, balance of payments, in an export-led-growth system gives a highly distorted picture of the internal purchasing power of national currencies.

Economic growth can no longer be defined as merely raising the GNP and per capita income. A major share of benefits of economic development is appropriated by the upper sections of the society, leaving the masses where they were or even worse off. In developing countries, thus, theories of development have produced greater benefits for the more advanced sectors of the community than for the marginal sectors resulting in the widening of gap between the rich and the poor. It was, therefore, felt that in case the benefits of development were to be equitably distributed, the focus has to be on people and societies and the Third World countries have to evolve their own pathways to development.

Man at the Centre of Development

The World Development Reports which, the World Bank brings out every year, particularly the two latest reports *Knowledge for Development*, 1998/99 and *Entering the 21st Century*, 1999/2000; the Human Development Reports by the UNDP since its launch in 1990 and the reports of a number of international agencies such as UNESCO—*Learning : The Treasure Within*, and a number of international conferences such as—UN Conference of Environment and Development in Rio in 1992, the International Conference on Population and Development in Cairo in 1994, and the World Summit for Social Development in Copenhagen in 1995 consider that people are the most valuable resources and the real wealth of a nation. The new paradigm puts man at the centre of development with the objective of creating good conditions for all to enjoy a long, healthy, and creative life. Human development is the end-economic growth and social sector development are the means. Higher economic growth is for producing more goods and services and for generating employment, and for reducing poverty, while social development is essential for the well-being or improving the quality of life. Development of social sectors has become integral part of the recent development strategies. More investment in social sectors such as health, education and nutrition sustains economic growth, however, social sector development also cannot be sustained in the absence of economic growth.

The failure of the dominant paradigm led to re-thinking about alternative strategies. The opening up of China, and her record of performance also had its impact on these strategies. One of the pioneering efforts in this direction is *The Poverty Curtain* (1976) of Mahbub ul Haq. Haq, who passed away recently, would be remembered as founder and Chief Architect of UNDP's Annual Human Development Reports (1989-95). In order that development efforts spread to vast majority of population. Haq favoured drastic restructuring of political and economic power relationship. Haq suggested : Growth in GNP often does not filter down, what is needed is a direct attack on poverty: the market mechanism is often distorted by the existing distribution of income and wealth, and is generally an unreliable guide to setting national objectives; new development strategies must be based on the satisfaction of basic human needs rather than on market demand; and development styles should be such as to build development around people rather than people around development.

Another Development

Today considerations such as human aspects of development, linked to the improvement in quality of life and equitable distribution of national income are imperative. Several significant initiatives, in transversing this distance from the concept of economic growth to human aspects of development emphasising participatory approach and fulfilment of basic needs of people are briefly recapitulated here.

The Dag Hammarskjold Foundation, Uppsala in its report : *What Now? Another Development (1975)* summarizes the basic new directions : Devélopment of every man and woman—of the whole man and woman—and not just the growth of things, which are merely means. Development geared to the satisfaction of needs beginning with the basic needs of the poor who constitute the world's majority; at the same time, development to ensure the humanization of man by the satisfaction of his needs for expression, creativity, conviviality and for deciding his own destiny.....Another development requires transformation of socio-economic and political structures that have long been identified. They include such fundamental steps as agrarian reforms, urban reforms, reforms of the commercial and financial circuits, redistribution of wealth and means of production as well as the redesigning of political institutions through, *inter alia*, decentralization with a view to ensuring democratization of the political and economic decision making power, promoting self management and curbing the grip of bureaucracies. As history shows, few of these transformations can be achieved without changing the power structure itself.

Sarvodaya Movement in Sri Lanka

The Sarvodaya Movement in Sri Lanka since its inception in 1958 has aimed at securing the common man's participation to the maximum possible level in the developmental exercise. The movement is dedicated to the resurgence of human values.

One of the remarkable aspects in the Sarvodaya Rural Development strategy is the 'discovery of an intelligible language to open up the *development dialogue* with the people. It has been the experience of the workers of Sarvodaya Movement that the planning aspect in this strategy is the discovery of an intelligible language to open up the development dialogue with the people. The planners who came from outside, whether with the seal of authority and power of the Central Government in their hands or other accredited representatives from International and National Organisations never understood what the rural people meant by the term 'Development'. The planners had their own definitions which the common villager did not understand. This language of the rustic villagers, on the other hand, was not understood by the planners and administrators.

In the words of Ariyaratne 'a serious attempt to discover an intelligible language common to both was never made'. The Sarvodaya Movement took note of the increasing disparity between the understanding of common people as to what development was about and the expectations of the privileged in society pertaining to development. In case of the common man development as related to him is directly concerned with the satisfaction of his basic human needs.

Since people have lost faith in the highly advertised big government plans coming down from bureaucrats, they are getting attracted to the movement, knowing very well that it is a non-governmental voluntary effort. Some of the Sarvodaya principles which are considered to be important for a national development effort and which encourage common man's approach to development are

1. While the fundamental human rights of every individual should be ensured without exception in the eyes of the law, the principal aim of any development effort should be to fulfil without delay the social, economic, cultural and spiritual aspirations of that segment of the society which stands lowest in it.
2. National development plans in the village should be drawn up, implemented and evaluated with the fullest participation of the people of the village.
3. National development should have its beginning within the village itself. All development plans should be made with the village taken as the Unit. Development in respect of constituencies and the districts should be undertaken by the coordination of those village Units. We call this 'development from the village upwards'.
4. The primary goal of local production activities should be to utilize the human and material resources available in the village, to meet the needs of the village people themselves.
5. Use should be made of appropriate village technologies and organizational structures which the villagers themselves can control.

Sustainable Improvement in Quality of Life

The disquiet with the concept of development led to several major efforts; one such effort was the report of the Brundtland Commission, *Our Common Future*. The report made it obvious that the contents of economic growth would have to change and even the consumption of material goods should be according to the scale of sustainability. The concept of sustainability has emerged from our awareness of the disastrous consequences of avaricious and unchecked exploitation of nature and our acknowledgement that its resources are limited. It is the basis of the survival of the environment, of society and that of the individual.

Development Tasks

Today development is invariably linked with other related issues—poverty, environment, literacy, population pressures and human rights. The issues related to development require interdisciplinary knowledge and inter-sectoral understanding of problems as well as integrated plans for action. As Nobel leaureate Amartya Sen points out: Equally important is to link the strategies of development to some thing more fundamental, in particular the ends of economic and social development. Why do we seek development? What can it achieve, if fruitful? How are the successes and failures of policies including the reforms of traditional policies to be judged?

On the first Independence Day Jawahar Lal Nehru had laid down broadly the parameters within which development had to be pursued—the ending of poverty and ignorance and disease and inequality of opportunity. In this context, Sen says : Economic growth is important but it is valuable precisely because it helps to eradicate deprivation and to improve capabilities and the quality of life of ordinary people. We must not make the mistake—common in some circles—of taking the growth rate of GNP to be the ultimate test of success, and of treating the removal of illiteracy, ill health and social deprivation, as—at best—possible means to that hallowed end. The first and the most important aspect of Nehru's listing of what we have to do is to make clear that the elimination of illiteracy, ill health, and other avoidable deprivations are valuable for their own sake—they are the tasks that we face. The more conventional criteria of economic success (such as a high growth rate, a sound balance of payments, and so forth) are to be valued only as means to deeper ends. It would, therefore, be a mistake to see the development of education, health care, and other basic achievements only or primary as expansions of human resources—the accumulation of human capital—as if people were just the means of production and not its ultimate end. The bettering of human life does not have to be justified by showing that a person with a better life is also a better producer.

The theories and perspectives of development from economic growth to equitable distribution of benefits of development to sustainable development and enhancement of quality of life and development as a part of human rights philosophy has been a most rewarding and exhilarating study of contemporary society. We shall continue to study various aspects of development in the context of specific subjects. Equally important would be to spell out role of communication in development and some of the important aspects of Development Communication.

The definition of development given by the North-South Commission has been broader than merely alleviation of poverty. Development means more human dignity, safety, justice and equality. The elimination of existing strong inequalities within society is central to successful processes. Equality is the value which is of decisive importance to successful modernisation which also means democratisation leading to breaking up of old social structures based on inherited positions.

Depending on national priorities the goals of development would naturally be different for different countries—one child family in China, creating computer culture in Singapore, ORT, clean drinking water and rural roads in India. Development in any particular country comprises those programmes and projects which receive top priority in the planning process of that country.

The new paradigm of development does not envisage the role of communication as that of magic multiplier of development, however, it is certainly envisaged to play a facilitative role in the process of development.

Although it may appear to be a truism, the importance of communication to human life cannot be overemphasised;

for without communication no society can exist, no social structures would survive and flourish. Communication not only means to communicate or pass on information—it also means community participation. The basic features of communication are

(a) Communication is a process for transmission of ideas, thoughts and feelings from one person to another;
(b) Communication is persuasive and seeks to obtain desirable response to what is being transmitted;
(c) Communication is a two-way process both vertically and horizontally, in a spirit of 'give and take' or 'send or receive'.

Wilbur Schramm who was one of the foremost scholars recognised the important role that communication could play in the development of Third World countries. His landmark book, *Mass Media and National Development, The Role of Information in the Developing Countries*, is the first major treatise on the subject. His introduction to the above book : The Human Meaning of Underdevelopment, which describes the two families—the Ifes living in West Central Africa and the Bvanis in South Asia, has been written with rare sensitivity and concern for human and social problems and challenges faced by the society in these countries. Schramm argues :

> Knowledge is better than ignorance;
> health is better than disease;
> to eat is better than to be hungry;
> a comfortable standard of living is better than poverty;
> to participate actively in one's nation is better than to be isolated from it.

The analysis of the problems of underdevelopment in the study provides us with an illuminating overview about the role communication can play in national development.

Some of the important conclusions of the study are reproduced below

1. National development moves very slowly in a climate where innovation is feared and distrusted, where fatalism leads men to believe they can do very little about their situation, where men do not believe in the dignity of labour and have little wish to better their lot...... this climate is to be modified. Wherever dangers or opportunities need to be reported, decisions need to be made, new knowledge needs to be taught—there information flows. Efficiency of communication is a consideration in determining the speed and smoothness of national development.
2. The whole information system, not a particular channel or a combination of channels, needs to be planned to fight the battle of development.
3. A developing country should try to make it as easy as possible to establish and maintain local media, such a small town newpapers and local radio stations. Local media are of great importance in social and economic development, not only because they are in a better position to know and serve the particular needs of a region, but also because they make it easier for more people to have access to media and therefore to take part in public affairs.
4. A developing country should try to establish a cooperative relationship between the organs of government responsible for its mass media development and education and other related activities. The development of education and literacy in a country has such an intimate relationship to media development that it is almost impossible to separate the two.

It is this anxiety as well as optimism that the potential of communication be utilised to further the cause of development, which has stimulated efforts to define and put in practice the concept of development communication. Since both the areas of study—development and communication by themselves elicit a large number of opinions, analysis, studies, any precise definition of development communication has eluded the communication and development scholars and experts. There has, however, been a broad agreement that development communication is primarily oriented to the needs of the people, implies a grass-root approach, and is decentralised and participative.

Development Communication

Development communication defies precise definition. It has been variously considered as a concept, approach, an ideal or even a philosophy. It also underlines certain amount of ideology, that of use of communication for development.

The term development journalism first cropped up around 1967 to define a notion of journalism according to which reporting events of national and international significance should be constructive in the sense that it contributes positively to the development of the country concerned. Its main focus should not be on day-to-day news but on long term development processes. Western models of journalism are seen as not transferable to developing countries (Michael Kunczik, *Concepts of Journalism*).

Whereas the two terms, development journalism and development communication are generally used by the communication scholars interchangeably, Shelton Gunaratne in paper—Old Wine in a New Bottle : Public versus Developmental Journalism in the US has said Developmental journalism has its roots in development communication which goes back to the work of agricultural extension carried out by large land grant state universities in the United States. Eventually it developed into a coherent doctrine.

The term development journalism as such was coined and introduced to international discussion at the Philippines University of Los Banos. In the early 1970s, the DEPTH-News a pioneer agency in development journalism defined it as "investigative reporting applied to the problems of development. It is not sunshine journalism."

Development communication emerged as a field of study during the post-World War II years when the countries of Asia, Africa and Latin America were asserting their right to independence, self-reliance and economic development. Its genesis is generally traced to the introduction and application of Agricultural Extension, also termed as Extension Education in most of the developing countries in early 1960s. The importance of communication as a tool to motivate and persuade people for eliciting positive response to various development programmes took shape. The use of Agricultural Communication became popular in some of the developing countries, giving rise to the use of the term (Rural Communication) in due course. It was soon realised that communication input cannot be confined to the development of agricultural aspects alone and also that apart from rural areas, urban areas also needed improvement and development. It was essentially an interplay of some of these factors that led to the emergence of the term development communication.

It is significant that the University of Philippines at Los Banos (which was the first University in the world to have Development Communication courses), retitled its Master's Degree programme in agricultural communication, as an M.A. in Development Communication. Thus, development communication is something with which the developing countries are already familiar in different forms like agricultural extension education or rural communication. The origins of development communication are, therefore, embedded in the practical efforts and situations of the developing countries in their tasks of changing the life styles, and improving the economic conditions of the people.

It is, however, more than agricultural extension education or rural communication. It does not restrict itself merely to the development of rural areas, nor is it concerned with agricultural development alone. It is oriented towards development whether it be in rural or urban areas or in agriculture, family planning, industrial production sectors.

One of the originators of the concept, Nora Quebral of the Los Banos University defines development communication as "the art and science of human communication applied to the speedy transformation of a country and the mass of its people from poverty to a dynamic state of economic growth that makes possible equality and the larger fulfilment of the human potential."

The above definition has been generally referred to, in any discussion about development communication by several media experts. Development communicaton uses communication media to help bring about socio-economic upliftment of the people in a way which are compatible with its humanistic goals. Quebral says : The very phrasing of development communication indicates its orientation towards goals, not to means. Its goals are inherent in the meaning given to development. Some of the more qualitative are the enhancement of quality of life, unfolding of human personality and humanisation of the individual. The humanistic goals, as well as the multifaceted nature of development (economic, social, political and cultural aspects) predict a wider scope for the study of the practice of development communication.

Mercado defines development communication as an "incremental process which starts with the diffusion of new information and technology which stimulates people to bring about conditions in the environment favourable to maximum productivity and the improvement of the general well-being." Rosario-Braid says that development communication requires communication personnel to go beyond their traditional roles. "The communicator's role will be that of enabling people to express their aspirations through available media and to assist them in attaining greater productivity". She says that in a broad sense, development communication is "the identification and utilization of appropriate expertise in the development process that will assist in increasing participation of intended beneficiaries at the grassroot level."

The function of development journalism is not merely

to keep a watch on government actions, but to promote the development of the country. Peter Golding wrote that development journalism could promote national progress by (1) stressing the educational function of news by raising the awareness of events and issues; (2) producing stories about social needs or problems in the hope of stirring up government action; and (3) highlighting self help projects that can be implemented by other communities and reporting on obstacles to development.

Development communication is said to cover every subject under the rubric "development" be it agriculture, environment, health care, literacy and education. A number of media experts have given many definitions ranging from simple to more elaborate.

According to J. F. Jamias, development journalism is characterized by the following five formalistically defined criteria :

1. Purposefulness (goal oriented)
2. Pragmatism (judged by results)
3. Relevance (to the development of the country)
4. Mass orientation (by addressing common problems)
5. Scientific outlook of development journalists.

The basic purpose of development journalism, as with other forms of journalism, is to inform, educate and entertain. Since people need basic information about the development programmes and plans envisaged by various departments of the government, information should be presented in an interesting and intelligible manner so that the intended beneficiaries are fully aware of all aspects.

Equally important function of development journalism is to investigate, analyse and interpret such plans. In the past, development journalism has been criticised for its tendency to depend wholly on government organisations, media officers, and others who, in the name of development news, tried to make propaganda even about those programmes which were not really useful for the people. Development news is not PR handout which presents list of success stories achieved by government in different areas. In a country like India where even after 52 years of independence, there are visible pockets of poverty and distress there would always be need for in-depth study and analysis of the failures, as well as successes.

Development journalism should seek to create an enabling environment, which through increased and accurate information facilitates the development process itself. It makes the expert knowledge available where it is needed and provides a forum for exchange of views and discussion. As Wilbur Schramm says : It is generally the increasing flow of information that plants the seeds of change. It is also the widened background of information that furnishes the climate for "nationness" itself. By making one part of a country aware of other parts...by making possible a nationwide dialogue on national policy, by keeping the national goals and national accomplishments always before the public, modern communication can help separate development into truly national developments.

Public Journalism

In my quest for understanding the very many nuances and dimensions of development journalism, I came across a review regarding emerging concept of public journalism in the United States which is very similar to the concept of development journalism that the West denounced during the debate on the New World Information and Communication Order (briefly referred to earlier on page 41).

Shelton Gunaratne, Professor of Mass Communication at the Moorhead State University in the above paper* refers to several research studies and postulates that public confidence in news dropped sharply (Between 1988 and 1993 people's confidence in television news dropped from 55 to 25 and newspapers news from 50-20 per cent)

* Old Wine in a New Bottle : Public versus Developmental Journalism in the USA, Shelton Gunaratne in *Asia Pacific Media Educator*, Vol. I :1, September, 1996.

because journalism in all forms ignores its obligations to effective public life and the failure has been a major contributor to the resultant malaise in public life. Journalism should be, and can be, a primary force in the revitalization of public life.

The terms public journalism, civic journalism and community journalism have been used interchangeably. He quotes Lambeth from his paper, Review of good news, social ethics and the press, about new forms of civic journalism constituting some combinations of the following :

Careful, timely and sensitive listening to public needs,
Systematic consultation of the public by means of polls and focus groups,
Journalist-organized dialogue with panels of resource specialists chosen for their differing expertise and perspectives,
Media sponsored public fora designed to deliberate on key issues,
Continuity of indepth reporting on issues chosen independently by journalists for their fidelity to citizen concerns,
Occasional cooperative projects by newspapers, radio and/or television newsrooms.

Communication and Participation

Since the very inception of planning process in India, participation of people in development programmes has been the sheet anchor of the development policy of the central and state governments. In recent years, however, the term participation has become an important part of the development lexicon. In spite of the enormous importance attached to this concept the term has not been clearly conceptualized. It is, therefore, becoming more of a rhetoric.

A common element in the lexiographic meanings of participation is the centrality of "sharing", e.g. entitling policy holders to a share of company's additional profits or like workers participation—the involvement of employees at levels in the policy making decision of a company. In the absence of genuine sharing of the benefits of development programmes, participation is being more and more sloganised rather than being implemented earnestly.

Communication, of course, is one of the key elements to achieve participation. The new development communication perspectives underline community orientation—community radio, community listening groups, etc., self management and self reliance, voluntary action and a right to participate in planning, implementation and decision making. This, however, does not mean that planners, managers and experts have no role to play in executing the development programmes. It is important that knowledge, experience and view point of the local people be given due consideration before decisions are arrived at. The beneficiaries of the development programmes be not considered as passive recipients, they should rather be taken as stake holders in the success of development process.

Whereas participation as a part of communication process has been enthusiastically accepted in most of the countries, participation of the people at grassroot level remains generally very low. In the case of mass media particularly as we shall see in subsequent chapters—participatory communication is a difficult task. Since administrators fear that participation may generate more expectations than may be ordinarily met, they see an element of risk in involving people in the development process.

The close relationship between development, participation and communication was appropriately conveyed by the UNESCO Director of Communication Division in his Key Note address at the AMIC 25th Anniversary Conference held at Singapore in June 1966; as under :

> The struggle against poverty, education for all, the preservation of the environment, the fight against AIDS, the promotion of human rights and of a culture of

peace, all these great and noble causes for which the international community is mobilizing its human, intellectual and financial resources, will remain idle words if the people directly concerned in the rural areas and in the suburbs of the megalopolis: do not themselves consider these causes as their own. Therefore, they should be given the means and the skills to participate in the communication process, in order to voice their opinions and aspirations through their own media or, at least, through media with which they can identify. There is no development without participation, as there is no participation without communication. Development, participation and communication form part of a continuum.

REFERENCES

Adler, H. J. (1973). The World Bank's Concept of Development. In : *Development and Planning*, Bhagwati, J. N. and Eckaus, R. S. (eds.). The MIT Press, Cambridge, Massachusetts.

Ariyaratne, A. T. (1980). Collected Works, Vol. II, Sarvodaya Research Institute, Sri Lanka.

Entering the 21st Century, World Development Report, 1999/2000. The World Bank, Washington.

Kunazik Michael (1988). *Concepts of Journalism, North and South*. Friedrich-Ebert-Stiftung, Bonn.

Many Voice, One World (1980). Report of the International Commission on the Study of Communication Problems, London, Kogan Page/UNESCO.

Rogers, E. M. (1976). *Communication and Development—Critical Perspectives*. Sage Publications, London.

Schramm Wilbur (1964). *Mass Media and National Development. The Role of Information in the Developing Countries*. Stanford University Press and UNESCO, Paris.

NOTE

Dr. A. T. Ariyaratne, the well known social thinker and founder President of Sarvodaya Shramadana Movement of Sri Lanka was presented the Gandhi Peace Prize-1996 by the President Dr. Shankar Dayal Sharma on 1 January, 1997.

3

Indian Communication Landscape

India, with one billion population, is a land of contrasts, a plural and a multi-lingual society. It has a wide range of communication media, extending from inter-personal methods of communication to satellite broadcasting, from a two-page broad sheet in a regional language printed on a treadle so common in small towns and villages even now, to multi-edition dailies printed through facsimile printing process, the second largest broadcasting service in the world, a burgeoning television and cable TV system and now the emerging multi-media and internet revolution in the urban areas and one of the largest film industries in the world.

In the ancient Indian society, religious, philosophical and cultural discourse was characterised by oral communication. Cradle of an ancient civilisation, India has also been a rich repository of traditional forms of communication. For thousands of years the Indian religious and social landscape was dotted with saints and scholars, wandering monks, priests and preachers who would move from one place to another and disseminate thoughts and ideas on various aspects of life, religion and social behaviour. Interestingly, even today vast congregations of men and women are frequently organised where modern day *gurus* and *rishis* expound religious discourses. These programmes receive fillip from the audio-visual media when these are further disseminated through different TV channels. This pattern of communication—a communication experience in itself—oral, interpersonal aided by the gadgets of electronic technology—extensive public address system, closed circuit TV has all the attributes and characteristics of the Indian communication process encompassing elements from the ancient to the modern media of communication.

Oral Communication

Speech is beyond doubt the most important vehicle of human communication. The culture of the Indian nation has been predominantly oral. The spoken word always had a sanctity of its own. It was revered as the source of knowledge and inspiration for good conduct. Before the advent of printing technology, traditional beliefs were disseminated orally. In ancient days oral communication was the only technique available to the religious preachers and philosophers for propagating their point of view.

Large masses of people were illiterate. The general masses were not aware of the advantages of literacy or education. Their outlook towards life was determined by fate and accident of birth. In such a situation the oral tradition of communication was harnessed to perpetuate ideas in support of the *status quo* and the social system prevailing at the time. The Brahmin priests used highly sanskritised language which carried an aura of scholarship and erudition. The religious teachings were confined to the elite, far beyond the access of the general masses.

Although the means of transport were primitive, communication by religious preachers was still possible. These religious preachers who were known as *parivrajakas* (wandering monks) travelled from and between various centres of pilgrimages and delivered discourses on religious matters, epics and scriptures. It will be interesting to point out the difference in the methods and use of language by the preachers of Brahminism and Buddhism. Whereas, the Brahmin priests used sanskritised, literary and scholarly language, the Buddhist method of communication was through local language. People were therefore more receptive to the Buddhist mode of communication.

During the modern times Mahatma Gandhi was one of the most successful practitioners of oral communication. In order to communicate his plans of action during freedom struggle his views and philosophy. Gandhi was not contented with his writings alone. He spoke with conviction and sincerity of purpose: his expressions were chosen with utmost care. His words and sentences were most appropriately chosen to convey his meaning. He used *Padayatra* (literally journey by foot: but also included journey by train) and prayer meetings for establishing direct and personal rapport with his listeners.

The other interpersonal channel which carried Gandhiji's message to the people was his regular prayer meeting. Silent prayer was followed by singing of hymns and chanting of Ramanam by the audience. These prayer meetings ended with a brief statement by Gandhiji on some vital issue. The regular national and international media looked forward to these statements from the greatest leader of the Indian freedom movement. Thus, the prayer meetings became a very potent means for the dissemination of the Gandhian ideas on politics, economics, village uplift, untouchability, *ahimsa*, *satyagraha* and *swadeshi* (Vilanilam, 1987).

Today, in spite of the vastly expanding media of mass communication, interpersonal communication through spoken word continues to enjoy a predominant position particularly in villages; the extension workers, political and opinion leaders rely on spoken word communication for the dissemination of the desired message and putting across their point of view.

Traditional Forms of Communication

Even where modern media have penetrated isolated areas, the older forms maintain their validity, particularly when used to influence attitudes, instigate action and promote change. Extensive experience shows that traditional forms of communication can be effective in dispelling the superstitions, archaic perceptions and unscientific attitudes that people have inherited as part

> of tradition, and which are difficult to modify if the benefits of change are hard to demonstrate. Practitioners of the traditional media use a subtle form of persuasion by presenting the required message in locally popular artistic forms. This cannot be rivalled by any other means of communication.
>
> *Many Voices, One World*

The traditional forms of communication constitute a potential source for conveying messages for economic and social development. Communities and individuals have utilized a wide range of media—local fairs, puppet shows, street theatre, folk songs and ballads for social purposes and as a support to local development schemes for health and family welfare campaigns, for creating political awareness.

In India, the most effective means of communication, specially in villages continue to be the traditional forms—folk theatre, folk tales, and of course, religious discourses. Folk forms which have been traditionally used as a means of disseminating information are diverse in nature and include different combinations of drama, dance, song, mime, story telling and puppetry.

India has a rich tradition of using folk media for nation building activities; even during the freedom struggle folk songs were used to popularise *satyagrah* and conveying political messages. Gurudev Rabindranath Tagore, in his famous *swadeshi samaj* speech in July 1904 advocated the use of *Jatra*, festivals and songs in order to reach the rural masses. Likewise, the eminent Tamil poet Subramanya Bharathi started using folk music to invoke patriotic feelings. Folk tunes were used to popularise songs on glories of spinning-wheel, need to boycott British goods and other diverse themes associated with the freedom struggle. Even during the recent parliamentary elections, *Jatra* was one of the popular modes used for campaigning.

The relevance of traditional form of communication—*Nukkad Natak* (street plays) was brought in bold relief when this form was utilised in states like Orissa, Uttar Pradesh and Bihar to apprise the rural population of the recent Kargil conflict. In this day and time, when there has been exponential growth in broadcast media and means of transport and travel are within the reach of common man; one is confronted with a sense of dismay that there would be some people in the rural areas of the country who would be still ignorant of the national happenings in the country. These street plays were perhaps one of the few successful channels to inform the people of various aspects of the conflict as also the valour and sacrifices made by the Indian soldiers. The plays were equally successful in instilling a feeling of patriotism in the audience.

The present author, never sure about the efficacy of folk media in transmitting development messages was pleasantly surprised when the participants of the Rural Press Seminar organized at Jaipur in 1994 were treated to a first rate performance by the folk artists in Lal Sot village near Jaipur. The artists, divided in two groups of singers, would take up one after the other through songs, the issues of corruption, maladministration and lack of development in the villages; and hold the elected representatives in the Panchayats and legislative assembly squarely responsible for the state of affairs. The performance not only entertained the audience through their presentation but also informed and educated them about the goings-on in the state politics. Nothing was considered sacrosanct, no body was above reproach; it was an open house performance with village people as participants. That was an example of traditional media being utilised for creating awareness amongst people about the problems and lack of progress in the rural areas with telling effect.

The outcome of various researches has established the importance of folk media in development communication. Traditional uses of folk media were primarily for entertainment, social communication and religious activity. These media have an element of motivational and persuasive communication. There have been sporadic efforts to involve folk media for conveying development messages through mass media agencies.

These efforts have not gone very far as a number of traditional media experts have expressed the view that presenting messages through folk media which is spectator-oriented would alienate these media from their basic philosophy and cultural setting.

Radio and television have added new dimensions to folk music, making different styles known outside their language area. The mass media have made people aware of the unexpected wealth of folk and tribal music and exposed musicians to the cultural diversity of India and folk musical styles live again for millions to be heard and viewed over a vast media network for all times. They have created a new interest in folk music, not only among the musicians and sophisticated audiences, but also among the people themselves. The effect of the renewed interest in folk forms among urban circles, brought about partly by the mass media agencies has given stimulus to folk music of different regions.

The Government of India set up a Song and Drama Division in 1954 for tapping the traditional and folk forms of the media for plan publicity. The Division has ten regional centres and nine sub-centres in different parts of the country. The Division also has tribal centre at Ranchi. The centre utilises the folk forms by the tribal artists from Madhya Pradesh, Bihar and Orissa. The basic idea in establishing this centre is to provide and encourage development of suitable programmes in tribal idiom and dialect. The Division puts up field programmes in coordination with other units of the Ministry of Information and Broadcasting, government departments and voluntary organizations. During 1997-98, the Division organised, mostly in rural and semi-urban areas, 37,000 programmes on broad national themes and government policies.

Much of social usage of folk medium has been related to preindustrial societies in which cultural expression has been primarily oral and essentially localized. Traditional performing arts are functional and interpersonal, have a contextual base and would be able to carry the message of change, development and growth. However, there have been differing opinions in India on the wisdom of using mass media to broadcast folk media for social and development purposes. Successful publicity through folk arts depends on a happy synthesis of writing skill (at the script level) and theatre skills (at the performance level).

However, creative or innovative talent in the governmental organisations is lacking. There is a severe dearth of talent and imagination also. That's why the productions remain essentially ineffective.

There is also the aspect of inadequate funds at the performance level. As a result average or below average troupes perform who fail to build up the required effect. The most important lacuna is the absence of commitment of the management. This aspect becomes conspicuous when we consider the fact that certain *Yatras* and "street dramas" performed by the Communist workers in Bengal are much better produced and presented than the ones by the governmental organisations (Pillai, 1998).

Interpersonal Communication

Interpersonal communication has been classified as 'word of mouth communication that occurs in face-to-face interaction between two or more individuals'. Some of the characteristics of interpersonal channels are : message flow tends to be two-way, amount of feedback readily available is high; are more effective when the attitude change is the goal of the source. Since the modern means of mass communication had not been in place till such time as printing was invented in the 15th century in Europe, vast majority of people lived within the context of their small village or tribal community with interpersonal communication being the main form of social contact. The International Commission for the Study of Communication Problems in its report says : Such interpersonal communication has been ever present, unceasing and specially within a small community, unrivalled in its importance. In the past it must have served to strengthen the values of comradeship and cooperation to counter-balance the fragmentation imposed by subjection to external authority. In any case, it has always had a socializing dimension, encouraging work, harmonious group living, banding together in the struggle against natural forces and in collective decision making. It remains an irreplaceable facet of human communication.

Interpersonal communication usually occurs in social situations, whereas the mass media inform decisions, interpersonal contacts support and legitimate them. Interpersonal influence is a two-way communication, the audience can talk back and convince itself. It is flexible, it is more trustworthy. If a goal of interpersonal communication is to achieve a changed attitude, to this end as a rule interpersonal communication is more effective than mass communication. The great advantage that the mass communication has over interpersonal communication is that of multiplier factor in circulating messages and information. With the rapid proliferation of mass media in India, the mass communication process is reaching out to larger number of people. However, the number of people to whom the mass communication process reaches out cannot be ascertained, and from whom the feedback is not immediately available. In the mass communication process, the active participation of the recipients is comparatively small. In this context, Melkote refers to Schramm as under : Only when communication can build itself into the social structure, is it going to show any real hope of extensive results. Only when media channels can mix with interpersonal channels and with organisation in the village, are you going to have the kind of development you will like.

The communication system in the People's Republic of China is a good example of this model. The mass media in this country work with and through a complex web of interpersonal channels and groups, feeding people with information they need and at the same time can feedback to the party cadres.

Several communication scholars have emphasized the more effective use of interpersonal communication in combination with media channels, in situations which call for reaching people with new ideas and persuading them to utilize these innovations. Rogers in his study, Mass

Media and Interpersonal Communication, enumerates media forum (small groups of individuals who meet regularly to receive a mass media programme and discuss the contents) to Canada, Japan, India, Nigeria, Ghana and Brazil, linked to radio or television as one such example. Such a media forum programme in India was Rural Radio Forum or *Charcha Mandals* which made farmers aware of agricultural and health innovations and encouraged them to try new ideas. These forums were later on discontinued as the government felt that these had fulfilled the objectives for which these were initially planned.

It, however, needs to be stated clearly that efficient use of media to bring about social change must take into account adequate knowledge of local culture. The new practices sought to be introduced should generally conform to the societal norms of the group or the unit. In India interpersonal channels, in combination with mass media, have been used effectively for conveying social and political messages to the people. This in fact is the most favoured communication method of reaching to millions of people in the shortest possible time. In the recent parliamentary elections this combination—political and public rallies were organised in large numbers including street corner meetings in towns and villages; and the news—at times even live coverage through television, was successfully utilised to get across to the people from all sections of society.

Mass Communication

Mass communication, or communication through mass media, has been an ever-evolving process since the invention of printing by Gutenberg in the 15th century in Germany. Several historians believe that the modern age of communication dates from the invention of printing. Printing was initially used for dissemination of knowledge and ideas through books.

The beginnings of press in India as a part of mass communication and to propagate news and views about the current happenings in the contemporary society are credited to James Hicky who published the first newspaper in India called "Bengal Gazette" in 1780. Since then the Indian press struggled for survival and growth during the British rule in the country, made significant contribution to the freedom movement and articulated the aspirations of the people. During this period several of India's top freedom fighters were excellent journalists and public leaders with mass following who were excellent communicators as well, chief among them were Mahatama Gandhi and Tilak.

Since independence the print media in the country has proven its resilience. The Indian press is characterized by pluralism and range of diversity in terms of socio-economic, linguistic and cultural interests. The press in India is one of the freest in the world and has emerged as a strong pillar of democracy and rights of citizens.

The print media at present continues to be in a state of buoyancy in terms of growth in circulation, number of newspapers as also the languages in which the newspapers are published.

Print Media

A country's press reflects the society it lives in, and the excessive space devoted in newspapers and magazines to politicians and political parties doings is a mirror of what excites the readers. The newspapers are full of politicians' election speeches and the minute details of elections and electoral politics. The politicians recycle their speeches times without number every day, the newspapers dutifully publish the same speeches day after day. This excessive preoccupation with politics of the country is a legacy from the freedom movement when the press played an important role in mobilising public opinion against the foreign rule. It has, however, been observed that during the recent years economic policy issues and financial reporting are getting due importance, primarily because of the policy of economic liberalisation introduced since 1991, bringing in its wake far reaching changes in the business and economic sectors.

The circulation of newspapers in India increased 20% in 1998 over the previous years despite the marginal fall in the number of publications registered during the year. According to the Registrar of Newspapers in India's Report, *Press in India 1998*, the growth in the print media in 1998 was 5.09 per cent over the previous years, it has registered an increase of 6.53 per cent in 1997. The circulation in 1998 was 12,68,49,500 copies compared with 10,57,08,191 the previous year.

The newspapers were being published in 100 languages and dialects including 18 national languages and English. Hindi continues to top both the numbers as well as circulation with 17,836 newspapers commanding a circulation of 5,72,89,398. The *Times of India* was the top multi-edition daily, followed by *Malayala Manorama*. The *Anand Bazar Patrika*, published from Calcutta, claimed the highest circulation during 1998 among the single edition dailies.

Significantly ABC has also pointed out that the circulation of newspapers continued to rise phenomenally. The total average net paid circulation certified by the Bureau over the past ten years had increased from an average of 25.9 million to 40.9 million copies*.

As literacy levels in India are relatively low at 52 per cent and the physical distances to cover are huge, it is indeed a challenging task for newspapers to tackle the problems of time and distance in a country of India's dimensions and diversities. In terms of total newspaper circulation, India is at third place after Japan and USA. Another interesting feature of the Indian press is that newspapers in the country are amongst the lowest priced anywhere in the world.

Newspapers cover a broad area which includes every conceivable subject from offering hard news to entertainment, analysis and interpretation. Politics is, however, a major obsession of the Indian press. Barring a few exceptions, serious journalism devoted to an understanding of human condition and of deeper

---

* *Times of India*, 29 September, 1999.

developmental concerns is at a major disadvantage. Newspapers are becoming more and more commercial and fiercely competitive in their approach, so different from the idealistic service inspired pre-independence period. The press has been captured by the big business: and dependence on revenue from advertisements is quite noticeable. The power and potential of the press, and the media as a whole in reaching out to the masses is quite perceptible.

Over the past few decades, the Indian press has witnessed a three tier growth. The mainline English language newspapers, published mostly from the metropolitan centres and state capitals, constitute the upper crust of the press. The English language press, catering to less than 5 per cent of the readers has a major share of advertising revenue because it is seen by the advertisers as aimed at the upper class clientele credited with purchasing power.

Leading Hindi and regional language newspapers, which during the past more than a decade have registered phenomenal increase in circulation, constitute the second tier of the Indian press. The statistics show that the domination of English language newspapers is receding, as more and more regional language papers from non-metropolitan areas are being published. The regional language press is increasingly making use of advanced means of telecommunication and printing technology.

The third tier of the Indian press is constituted of the small newspapers, mostly in Hindi and Indian languages, are brought out from district centres, having grass-root contacts. This segment of print media has progressed rapidly because of the three factors—gradual spread of literacy, rise in people's pruchasing power and increasing level of political and general awareness and interests in the affairs of the country.

Interestingly there has been general scepticism regarding the useful purpose that host of small district newspapers serve. It would, however, be worthwhile even after more than 34 years of the publication of the book, *Communication and Change in Developing Countries*, to refer to the assessment about the district newspapers. and their contribution in encouraging local participation and mobilizing local effort : I have regarded these district papers as of immense value, for they focus the attention of the local population on local development effort and assist in creating interest in the local affairs. I personally know of a number of cases in which these small newspapers have exercised considerable influence on local administration and have helped to build local opinion on political and economic issues. If development requires local participation, these district papers have to play an important role in mobilizing local effort. It may be conceded that all of them are not motivated by the highest ideals, and some of them may be instruments of local politicians, but as a whole they are of great assistance to local development. Political decentralization and establishment of Panchayati Raj have created a new political structure in local administration. The Zila Parishads and Panchayat Samitis have been entrusted with wide powers in the spheres of local administration and local development. The small district newpapers have the same significance in local affairs as provincial papers in state matters and metropolitan papers in national problems.

Responding to the demands and requirements of its readers, the language press has evolved its own pattern. It accords proper importance to local and regional news as compared to national and international news which is generally received through news agencies. The events, problems and region specific news, which are generally not treated adequately by the metropolitan press are of special interest to the language press.

An emerging feature of the language press is the single daily domination in several states with circulation ranging from one-third or more of total circulation, and readership from half or more of the total readership in the language of the State. These States include Andhra Pradesh, Gujarat, Punjab, West Bengal and Kerala. Infact, in Andhra Pradesh, *Eenadu* dominates with half of total circulation and over 90 per cent of total readership in the State. In Kerala and Gujarat, two dailies have been dominating, both with significant share in circulation and readership as indicated in Table 1.

TABLE 1
States with Dominant Newspapers

State	Newspaper	In per cent	
		Share in total circulation	Share in total readership
A. P.	Eenadu	55	92
Gujarat	Gujarat Samachar	38	58
	Sandesh	30	47
Karnataka	Prajavani	26	57
Kerala	Malayala Manorama	42	63
	Mathrubhumi	31	54
Punjab	Punjab Kesari	37	50
Rajasthan	Rajasthan Patrika	34	50
Maharashtra	Navakal	8	27
	Lokmat	6	26
Tamil Nadu	Dinathanthi	18	66
	Dinamani	7	20
West Bengal	A. B. Patrika	24	45

Source : ABC : *Vidura*. Jan.-March 1999, p. 36.

The language newspapers, closer as they are to the local communities, reflect the cultural and social traditions of the people they serve.

Because of the highest rate of literacy in the country, the people of Kerala enjoy a high degree of awareness and can therefore claim a large slice of language press. The country's highest circulated daily paper, the *Malayala Manorama*, enjoys a high level of prestige in terms of editorial quality, introduction of latest printing technology and taking initiative in promoting agricultural and rural development in the state. A multi-edition newspaper, it has been the daily with highest circulation in the country for several years.

Electronic Media

Over the years and particularly so during the preceding two decades, India has developed a fairly extensive electronic media infrastructure. Radio and television, and cable television since the advent of gulf war in 1991, have seen exponential growth in terms of reach and impact. Presently, All India Radio network comprises 195 radio stations. The flagship of Doordarshan—the Primary channel—operates through a network of 897 terrestrial transmitters of varying powers to make available TV signals to over 87 per cent of population*.

Radio, which continues to be a very important medium, has not matched the growth of television. It is indeed a sad commentary on the priorities of government media planners in our country that radio, which has been the most widely used medium for development purposes, is cost effective and has the capacity to reach large audiences, has been marginalised.

The well-known radio personality, Mark Tully making a comparison between radio and TV says : Radio, as a means of mass communication is friendly and has a far bigger reach. When you are listening to radio, you are personally involved, your mind is working. This is because mind is picturising the piece of information being communicated. In television, it is like spoon feeding your audience. The pictures are there before you and voice over is nothing more than captions to a series of visuals.

There could not have been more unequivocal and categorical assertion about utilitarian qualities of radio than what has been stated in the UNESCO report on communication—*Many Voices, One World*. In developing countries, radio is the only medium that can really be labelled mass where a large proportion of the population can be reached by radio broadcasts and possesses the means to receive them. No other medium now has the potential to reach so many people so efficiently for information, educational, cultural and entertainment purposes. Radio can be used easily and economically to reach outlying regions and for communication in the many vernacular, often unwritten languages, existing in developing countries. Almost all countries have a certain

---

* India 1999.

capacity to produce radio programmes in line with their political needs, cultural patterns and basic values.

In the above context, one cannot help recalling the observations made by the Working Group on Autonomy for Akashvani and Doordarshan that India should have given first priority to the development and densification of radio for atleast next 10-15 years. Radio is far cheaper and the availability of cheap transistors has made it ubiquitous.

In the beginning of the nineties, the sudden arrival of satellite channels had affected the popularity of radio and it remained virtually dead, at least in urban areas. With the opening of FM channels, introduction of new programmes and application of latest technologies, the radio is fast coming back in the reckoning.

Radio continues to be most frequently used mass medium in development programmes. Development broadcasting originated primarily to carry information on agriculture and rural development, health and family welfare. Some of the important programmes where AIR has been making significant contribution are : radio support for distance education programmes launched by universities, schools and other organisations, pulse polio immunisation campaign, and in the broadcast of Radioscope, National Science Magazine started since April 1995. These programmes, as well as others concerning rural development and other sectors, would come up for detailed discussion in the respective chapters.

Radio is essentially a people oriented medium, a medium of the poor man, who is central to all the development strategies of the national and state governments. It is non-elitist and is ideally suited for dissemination of information at the local/community level. It would, therefore, be appropriate to briefly refer to India's experience in setting up the first local radio station at Nagercoil in 1989; as well as the lead taken by a Bangalore based media NGO, *Voices* and initiating the first ever community radio programme from Shimoga district in Karnataka.

The broad outlines of the initiative were finalized at

the International Consultation on Media Policy and Community Radio organised in September 1996 at Bangalore. The outcome of the Consultation was embodied in a valuable document—Bangalore Declaration on Community Radio. The Declaration states : Community radio is public service broadcasting in its most decentralised form. A community radio station serves a defined geographical area of a village or groups of villages, and is owned and managed by organization serving a given community. Such a radio station would, besides educating and entertaining people, connect people with people through participatory or circular communication, connect with organizations and communities, and finally connect people with government and public service agencies. In a number of ways community or public interest broadcasting can be termed Equal Opportunity Broadcasting, which is essential not only for effective democratisation of a public resource but also in the context of our plural society with a multiplicity of languages, cultures and ethnic groups. In terms of programming the community radio stations will build linkages between private broadcasters, local self-government institutions, educational and professional bodies and special interest groups. It is important that these groups are provided access to the medium in order to serve the public interest in all its dimensions Community radio stations should also work in concert with government agencies in reaching out to and promoting economic and social welfare of the marginalised and disadvantaged groups within the community.

Television made its beginning in the country as a modest pilot project in September 1959; when the President Dr. Rajendra Prasad inaugurated the Experimental Television Service, operated from improvised studio. The programmes were telecast twice a week for a duration of one hour each and the signals were limited to 25 km from Delhi. The regular service with a news bulletin was started in 1965.

It would be interesting to recall, in retrospect the delay in starting television in India was due to the general feeling in the government that television was a luxury, a status symbol with limited utility and, therefore, could not be treated on priority for allocation of funds in a poor country like India where the need was pressing for more important necessities for the people. However, the role of television from the very beginning as an aid to education and social change was clearly recognised. There was also a realization of the immense potential of television as an instrument of rapid socio-economic transformation.

Today Doordarshan, the National Television Service in India, is also one of the largest terrestrial networks in the world. The flagship of Doordarshan—the Primary Channel—operates through transmitters of varying powers to make available TV signals for over 87 per cent of population. Doordarshan uses a large number of transponders of the Indian National Satellite. Doordarshan programmes are watched by 350 million viewers in their homes. During 1997-98, Doordarshan earned around Rs. 5 billion as revenue through commercial advertisements. It has its production facilities in 42 cities across the country.

TABLE 2
Pattern of Increase in Television Transmitters and TV Households

Year	No. of transmitters	No. of TV households (in millions)
1980	18	-
1985	172	6.8
1990	519	27.8
1995	672	52.3
1996	743	-
1997	868	57.7
1998	1027	63.2

Source : Doordarshan 1997 and Doordarshan 1998 (Prasar Bharti Broadcasting Corporation of India).

To meet the regional aspirations, 10 regional language satellite channels on Doordarshan were introduced in 1994. Since the footprints of INSAT satellites cover the whole country, regional language programmes are available throughout the country regardless of one's place of residence.

The Satellite Instructional Television Experiment (SITE)

in 1975, was primarily undertaken to experiment with television through satellite communication to broadcast special programmes in 2400 villages in six states aroused wide international interest. Subsequently the Ninth Asian Games in 1982 proved to be a significant milestone in the growth of Indian television because it heralded the introduction of colour television in the country. In 1983, a Special Plan for television expansion was approved. The plan was historic because beginning July 1, 1984, one transmitter was commissioned every day for a period of almost four months. During 1984, India's first soap opera *Hum Log* was introduced with the object of promoting women's welfare, family planning and reinforcing positive social values. The programme became very popular and made headway for other serials.

The Gulf War coverage by CNN in 1991 was a defining moment in the beginning of a new era in television broadcasting in India which ushered in far-reaching changes at a dizzy place. This was also the beginning of multi-channel TV in the country. The Special Edition of *India Today*, caught the spirit of the moment when it heralded the arrival of CNN in January and of STAR TV in April 1991, as "easily the most dramatic revolution took place on the TV screen. 1991 was the year when India ended decades of isolation from the rest of the world". Subsequently also the fortnightly news magazine wrote

The mundane television set has suddenly turned into an incredible technicolour dream boat.... and like a lost tribe discovering an oasis in the desert, lakhs of Indians are hot wired into this superbazaar of soaps, sports, news, music, sex and much more....Hungry for any kind of news or entertainment, lakhs of people in cities and towns across the nation are now only too familiar with the names of the new electronic media companies, an alphabet soup of initials promising round the clock entertainment—MTV, CNN, BBC, ATN, Zee TV.

If any thing, the number of satellite channels has increased rapidly. The Sengupta Committee, while referring to Satellite channel universe, lists 52 channels operating in the country.

Today TV is no longer an urban phenomenon. Its penetration, in the sub-urban and mofussil areas, and even in villages, is not considered a big deal any longer. There has, in fact, been a virtual paradigm shift from state monopoly of electronic media to virtual *laissez faire*; from the position of monopoly national broadcaster to one of the players is indeed a metamorphosis in the media landscape in the country. What does this metamorphosis augur for channelising communication media for development purposes?

Television was started in India for the purpose of development communication as a vehicle of social change and national cohesion by unhesitatingly upholding progressive values and involving the community in a free dialogue, but it has gradually steered away from the enshrined development goals and chartered a course contrary to its development pursuits. Today entertainment has become the primary function of this medium.

The Working Group on Software for Doordarshan, under the chairmanship of P. C. Joshi (1982) indicated : Today development and communication are entirely unrelated. On the one hand, we have a powerful medium like Doordarshan not being used for development task, on the other hand we have developed programme and action without any media or communication support. The two should work hand in hand, reinforce each other if planning has to be effective. The Group also expressed its unhappiness on the VIP orientation of the programmes and said : It is a pity that a television system which is not only publicly funded but is also directly run by the government. on the ground that is necessary to make television serve the purpose of development in the direction of socialism, should show so little orientation towards the common people in its news and current affairs programmes. Doordarshan news should be gathered and presented from perspective not only of the government, the ruling party and the urban well-to-do, but also of the many other social, economic and political groups, who constitute the nation.

The Indian television industry has become completely

entertainment oriented; telecast of feature films, *chitrahar*, soaps and other serials has made Indian TV a tool of entertainment with development being relegated to a subordinate slot. Television commenced with the aim of promoting socio-economic development of rural people by disseminating of knowledge, through education and information. During the course of expansion, however, Doordarshan now fulfills the three widely accepted principles : entertainment first, information second, and education last. The entertainment element has gone increasing at the cost of education and information dissemination.

Doordarshan, despite its great potential to communicate for millions of the illiterates, has its own constraints. Being mainly a unichannel operation, in most of the cities, it has to satisfy its viewers by compromising on its declared objectives. It is far behind in rural development communication, as the urban viewers, being in majority, can lobby and exert pressure to get the balance tilted in favour of entertainment programmes. Almost all the production centres of Doordarshan are located in cities and most of the programme producers have an urban background. Majority of the participants in its programmes are drawn from urban areas. Naturally rural issues are least projected.

Many programmes related to development subjects are broadcast regularly which bring about consciousness among the people. Educational programmes prepared by UGC, NCERT, etc. and agriculture broadcasting are good examples of development communication. Programmes based on health, environment, science and technology, etc. are also telecast from time to time. But these programmes contain many drawbacks including elitist nature. Similarly, the programmes on social awareness also need many improvements.

Development programmes are shabbily produced. They lack aesthetics and necessary visuals. Dull production leaves the viewer cold. Development programmes are never telecast on prime time and they fail to attract advertisement revenue. The viewers often consider such programmes as government propaganda and surf channels. TV can be most effective medium of mass communication only if it provides good programmes.

There has been pervasive concern over the impact of advertising on the quality and contents of the television programming at various levels; it has unleashed the forces of consumerism; which is spreading like wildfire, whereas access to the basics of life remains a serious problem for a large number of population. Several studies, seminars and reports of working groups have expressed concern that in order to meet the requirement of sponsors and advertisers, TV channels telecast programmes which threaten family values and usher in a life style out of sync with the Indian traditions. Suggestions have been in place to find solution to this situation which is becoming more and more intractable issue.

Public Service Broadcasting has been one such recommendation which has been put forward in the report of Subcommittee of the Consultative Committee for the Ministry of Information and Broadcasting on National Media Policy and the Working Group set up to review the provision of Prasar Bharati Act; both these reports were submitted in 1996.

The Consultative Committee recommended : The national broadcasters should bear the responsibility to offer a high quality public service broadcasting that informs, educates and entertains the people. It also recommended : Adequate care should be taken to enable the setting up of non-commercial broadcasting stations to be run by universities, educational institutions, panchayats/local bodies, State governments, etc. Likewise, the Working Group said : This Group believes that Prasar Bharati as the inheritor of the great tradition should be the quintessential public service broadcaster. This is not to suggest that private broadcasters have no role to play in this sphere. Indeed, the private operators should have an obligation to put out programmes devoted to socially relevant themes and earmark certain slots for the purpose. The public service broadcasting manifesto, propounded by the first Director General of BCC, John Reith says

> The service must not be used for entertainment purposes alone. Broadcasting had a responsibility to bring into the greatest possible number of homes in the fullest degree all that was best in every department of human knowledge, endeavour and achievement. The preservation of high moral tone—the avoidance of the vulgar and the hurtful—was of paramount importance. Broadcasting should give a lead to public taste rather than pander to it.

At times, these views of Reith have been criticised as paternalistic. Whereas there has been a large body of support for the ethos of public service broadcasting, it has been showing signs of crisis in this era of deregulation and commercialization. It would of course be readily accepted that dangers of deregulated system must be encountered by putting in place suitable measures. In Britain, Broadcasting Standards Council (BSC) was established in 1988 to act as a focus for public concern about the portrayal of violence, and sex, and about standards of taste and decency. The BSC monitors programmes, examines complaints from the public and undertakes research. The BSC has drawn up a code of practice which the BBC and other broadcast bodies are legally obliged to reflect in their own codes of conduct.

In India, we have to go a long way in putting in place such regulatory measures, and more importantly implementing these meaningfully and sincerely. We will have to ensure media professionals, researchers, civil society, voluntary groups and NGOs—proper initiative, so that new space could be created for public service broadcasting and community media; adequate funding be provided—properly regulated government allocations, a tax on advertising revenue, may be subsidy to production houses for producing educational and developmental programmes.

Multi-media Communication

In the Indian context which has a rich tradition of oral and traditional communication and a vibrant print and electronic media. Internet has emerged as an important factor in the fast developing communication landscape. With internet expanding rapidly the Information Age is well and truly upon us. The worldwide web is a challenge because of the interactive opportunity it offers for instant communication and is racing ahead at a breath taking speed. A large number of newspapers are available on internet. *The Hindu* was the first Indian newspaper to go on the net in 1995. Soon, other newspapers, both in English and Indian languages followed suit as also magazines. As is the predominant practice, the world over, access to Indian newspapers is also free. A major newspaper group chain operating from the capital has sites for all its publications, as well as for classifieds, jobs and careers, property, education, computing, etc. All these sites are easily available. It also offers Web Directory which has 9000 websites on Art and Culture, Business and Economy, Health and Fitness, News and Media, People and Society, etc.

Internet access in India has not reached a critical mass yet in view of the limitations of the infrastructure and bandwidth. Ever since the internet space was deregulated by the government, the number of internet subscribers is growing. Till date there are more than 2.5 lakh internet subscribers in India and according to a report there will be a quantum leap in the next twentyfour months. More than 2 million internet subscribers are expected by the end of 2001.

This technology is impacting print media as well. More and more online editions of newspapers will be available. Colour and graphics will play an increasingly important role in newspaper publishing. The newspapers will become increasingly digital in its production processes.

Another India? The other face of India, far different from the wandering monks depending upon oral communication in hoary days of distant past.

Non-dominant Communication

Non-dominant communication processes are media forms,

which run contrary to dominant values, ideological propositions and organisational norms. Dominant communication consists of those media processes which have been marginalised by the homogenizing zeal of an industrial economy, and which are largely sustained through an intrinsic local ethos in addressing social issues of the moment.

These forms, amorphous and scattered as they are, may include street theatre based on folk songs and puppetry to convey messages of social importance, write ups and feature stories on important contemporary issues which the mainstream media may not take up (or would take up only when the issue has been articulated through non-dominant processes) and has already become important enough to receive attention at a regional or national level. The way the issues concerning Narmada dam were articulated through the vernacular press at the local level before these found space in the national press, cyclostyled bulletins, leaflets and later on video films, were all instances and forms of non-dominant communication used for serving an important purpose. These processes have provided several feminist groups and voluntary organisations means to express their point of view and represent the ideology these stand for. The noted free lance journalist, Bharat Dogra, who publishes *News from Fields and Slums*, has found a novel method to articulate his views on poverty, environmental problems and concerns of the common person. He finds that small booklets, 16-32 pages, economically priced helps him focus on an issue and create the necessary impact. The production costs are low; he has managed to carry on the *News* with financial support from his wife, who later on joined him after giving up her government job. He has been, on principle, opposed to foreign funds, and hopes the feature service will motivate the next generation to create necessary climate wherein issues concerning the poor and slum dwellers could be properly focussed.

This is in fact the spirit behind non-dominant communication processes.

REFERENCES

Lerner and Schramm (1967). *Communication and Change in Developing Countries*. East-West Center Press. University of Hawaii. Honolulu.

Malik. Madhu. *Traditional Forms of Communication and Mass Media in India*. Documents on Communication and Society-13. UNESCO.

McQueen, David (1998). *Television : A Media Students Guide*, Arnold. London.

Melkote, Srinivas, R. (1991). *Communication for Development in the Third World—Theory and Practice*. Sage Publications, New Delhi.

Pillai. N. N. (1998). Communication through Folk Art Forms. In : *Issues in Communication, The Basic Concepts*, J. S. Yadava and Pradeep Mathur (eds.), Kanishka Publishers, New Delhi.

Seminar (455). Alternatives in Communication. July 1997.

Vilanilam, John V. (1987). *Religious Communications in India*, Vol. I, Kairali Books International, Trivandrum.

Vir Bala Aggarwal (1999). Role and Contribution of Language Press in India, *Communication Today*, 3 (3), Jaipur.

NOTE

The section on Non-dominant communication is based on the papers included in *Seminar* (455).

4

Literacy, Education and Distance Learning

The issues of literacy and education have come up on the national agenda of the country during the closing decade of the present century as never before. Several international organisations including UNDP, UNESCO, the World Bank and human rights organisations have also highlighted literacy as being one of the significant factors which contributes towards improving the quality of life.

Literacy

In their book, *India : Economic Development and Social Opportunity*, Jean Dreze and Amartya Sen point out : Literacy is a basic tool of self defence in a society where social interaction often involves the written media. An illiterate person is that much less equipped to defend herself in court, to obtain a bank loan, to enforce her inheritance rights, to take advantage of new technology, to compete for secure employment, to get on the right bus, to take part in political activity, in short to participate successfully in the modern economy and society. Similar things can be said about numeracy and other skills acquired in the process of basic education. The basic education is also a catalyst of social change.... the spread of education helps to overcome the traditional inequalities of caste, class and gender, just as the removal of these inequalities contributes to the spread of education. Literacy obviously helps people to understand the functioning of the system, to deal with the government bureaucracy, to be aware of their rights, to understand and tackle new problems, and to achieve other abilities that are important for an effective role in local politics.

For an illiterate person, acquiring capability to read and write has a fascination of its own. It not only imbues him with a sense of self-worth, and confidence, it opens for him vistas of opportunities outside the confines of his limited environment. In this context Wilbur Schramm makes certain meaningful observations : Print, when one learns to read, is not only a source of much pleasure, but also a source of understanding of many problems in the world. Even beyond that literacy is not just learning how to read but is concerned with comprehending a form of reality beyond immediate experience. Print, therefore, is a liberating revolutionary experience; it helps free an individual from his group, his social customs, his routine.

It is now accepted that literacy has great potential to make life significant, interesting and indeed full. According to contemporary thinking literacy is one of the cultural areas considered essential for human development and illiteracy and poverty are considered to be the two sides of the same coin. It has also been incorporated as a part of physical quality of life index (PQLI). This index was based on three factors : infant mortality rate, life expectancy at the age of 1 year, and the literacy rate of adults. Each factor was indexed on a scale of 0 to 100—0 being the worst performance recorded among the nations of 1950, and 100 the best performance to be expected anywhere by the year 2000. The Overseas Development Council, however, ceased publication of the PQLI in 1990. The torch was immediately taken up by the UN Development Programme, which has published its Human Development Index annually since 1990. In its version for 1994, HDI used life expectancy at birth as its health component. The educational element was a combination of adult literacy (given a weight of two-thirds) and the mean number of years of schooling received (a weight of one-third). The Human Development Report 1996 introduced a new multi-dimensional measure of poverty—the Capability Poverty Measure (CPM). The CPM is an index of lack of three basic capabilities as under :

(i) The capability of living a healthy and well-nourished life-represented by the proportion of children under five who are under weight.
(ii) The capability of safe and healthy reproduction represented by the proportion of births unattended by trained health personnel.
(iii) The capability of being literate and knowledgeable represented by proportion of women aged 15 and above who are illiterate.

To measure the capability poverty of a nation these three variables are added together and divided by three. The lower this simple arithmetic mean indicates the less capability poverty. The three variables in CPM are given equal weight because one capability cannot be a substitute for another.

India has the dubious distinction of being the country with the largest adult illiterate population in the world (over four times the population of UK) and the collective literacy rates of the South Asian region are the lowest in the world. It also has the largest number of children out of primary school (over twenty per cent of the global total). Some of these facts have been highlighted in *Human Development in South Asia* 1998 by Mahbub ul Haq. The Report also highlights the long distance India has travelled since independence: adult literacy rate has nearly tripled rising from 18 per cent in 1951 to 52 per cent in 1995. The Report points out : The quality of many primary schools is appallingly low; one in five children is over or under-age; one in three children drops out before completing the primary cycle; and one in two children does not have access to clean drinking water at school, according to survey evidence. A recent study in rural India found that not a single grade 5 student had mastered grade 2 competencies in Hindi or mathematics.

The vulnerable groups are often deprived of educational opportunities. The literacy rate in India varies from 90 per cent for rich urban males to a mere 17 per cent for poor, rural, scheduled caste women. The difference between the primary enrolment rate of landless peasant households and medium to large scale landowners is almost 20 percentage points.

The education profile of India varies considerably from state to state, with educational progress depending on political commitment—not economic resources. The best example remains Kerala, which has a literacy rate of 90 per cent but an income of around $ 1,000 (in PPP terms), compared to Punjab which has a literacy rate of only 60 per cent despite an income of over $ 2000. Educationally backward states must learn from India's educational high achievers. At present, about three quarters of out-of-school children live in just six states—Andhra Pradesh, Bihar, Madhya Pradesh, Rajasthan, Uttar Pradesh and West Bengal.

The third anniversary issue of *Outlook*, 19 October 1998, *Another India*, looks at the condition of majority of Indians who constitute the nation's rural poor in terms of food availability, drinking water, health care and education. Even according to the government statistics more than half of rural India is unlettered and seven of every ten village women are uneducated. And some one who went to school ages ago and remembers nothing, relapses into illiteracy, is also listed as literate. The reality of a village school teacher's life does not offer him encouragement to innovate or build rapport with either the children or the community. The feature on education enumerates the life of a village school teacher as : very few among those who plan education policies and allocate funds seem to know of the physical reality of a village teacher's life. He walks miles to get to his work place, trudges hours to get his salary, works without blackboards, chairs, tables, bathrooms, water and sometimes even a classroom. Naturally the teachers feel demotivated. Consequently the quality of education in the rural areas suffers.

The literacy movement in the country has already

shown the potential to develop into a movement beyond literacy. The nodal agency for this purpose, the National Literacy Mission (NLM) was inaugurated in May 1988. The emphasis of the Mission was on environment creation and more intensive training. The most important development which has taken place under the NLM is the prominence given to the campaign mode in the adult education programmes in the country. The success of Ernakulam and Kerala experiments for achieving full literacy has made these campaigns as unique experiments and distinguished these from other such programmes.

The Earnakulam District Total Literacy Campaign (TLC) was the first district level movement of its kind in India. It established a method for literacy campaigns in the districts of the state and proved to be a trend setter for such programmes in the country. The programme was spearheaded by Kerala Sastra Sahitya Parishad (KSSP) in the field of literacy from 1977 onwards. The KSSP mastered the technique of mobilising people in a very large way through *Kalajathas* and other media and itself grew into a mass organisation. It was only because of sustained and consistent efforts of organisations like KSSP and people's mobilisation that Kerala was declared fully literate on 18 April 1991. In a pamphlet *Make Literacy Work : A People's Movement*, it was argued : No programme will succeed without people's support... In all the countries which have achieved universal literacy one can see the support of the entire people for the movement. It is the failure to attract the attention of the mass of people that is the cause of the lack of success of literacy programmes in our country If they degenerate into ordinary official activity carried out for the sake of a government job, nothing can save them. It should be possible to convert literacy-work into a big people's movement.... The literates and the illiterates, individuals and organizations, school students and vice-chancellors...all can participate in this...

The work and contribution of KSSP has attracted worldwide attention because the KSSP activists have been important organizers of total literacy campaigns in different parts of the country. TLCs have been launched in 442 districts of the country covering an estimated 147 million illiterate persons and 230 districts have commenced post-literacy campaigns to consolidate the gains of literacy.

India is one of the few developing countries which has not allowed the expenditure on education to shrink during the reform period. Several landmark decisions to improve the levels of achievements in schools include:involvement of community and Panchayati Raj institutions (73rd and 74th constitutional amendments), creating parental awareness and ensuring minimum levels of learning. The 83rd Constitutional Amendment Bill has been introduced in the Rajya Sabha to make right to education a fundamental right and a fundamental duty.

Education

In terms of human development objectives, education is an end in itself, not just a means to an end. Education which is a basic human right, is critical for economic and social development. It is crucial for building human capabilities and for opening opportunities. Regarding the disappointing state of education in South Asia, Mahbub ul Haq, says : Education is the true essence of human development. Without education, development can be neither broad based nor sustained. Unfortunately, this is a lesson which South Asian development planners have still to learn.

The report of the Brundtland Commission, *Our Common Future* added urgency to the concept of sustainable development, which is generally understood to be used only in terms of environmental protection. According to contemporary thinking sustainable improvement in the quality of life becomes the central focus for policy making in all countries; and therefore, highest priority should be accorded to meeting the basic minimal survival needs of the population. It has also been stressed that the capital invested in people's health and education becomes an important economic factor. This sort of capital as against the earlier definition of capital (as investment in economic goods for increasing production) can be sustained by raising the level of investment in education, health and other social services. The Jomtien Declaration on *Education for All (1990)* introduced an additional element calling for right to life long education and training. During the closing decades of the present century, rethinking on all aspects of education—alongwith other important facets of development—has broadened our understanding of the vast dimensions of education as a process, as a factor encouraging an individual to participate in the political and social life of the community and the country, as well as an instrument for the empowerment of the women and disadvantaged sections of the population. One such dimension : Education is no longer seen as a fixed stage in life, beginning at about five years of age and continuing through primary, secondary and possibly tertiary level and ends once employment begins. In case we wish to achieve the full potential of education to solve the social and economic problems, and also that of an individual to rise up to his full capability and genius. We will have to give up this limited view. That is why learning is becoming a life long process and age is considered no bar to improve one's academic, technical and professional prospects and attainments. Information technology, innovations and improvements have also made it feasible to study at one's own pace—Open Learning Systems which would include Open Schools and Open Universities and now Virtual classroom and Virtual universities have made the pursuit of life long learning a real possibility.

The scope, role, as well as expectations from education system have also expanded vastly. The Government of India brought out a comprehensive document on education in August 1985, *Challenge of Education—a policy perspective*, which says : In addition to developing the personal attributes, education has to assume the responsibility for imparting knowledge about concepts and facts relating to different subjects and for developing skills in the area of languages and communication, as also interest in hobbies, games and sports.

Besides in relation to economic development and employment, education has to equip the pupils with competence, in terms of knowledge and skills, in various combinations at different levels of understanding, relating to the opportunities of employment in the context of a particular pattern and rate of development. Education has to play an important role in integrating the individual into the social system. It is also meant to indicate suitable habits for health care, mental application, management of time and conservation of physical, mental and emotional energy.

Today, besides the integration of the individual into the social system, it is equally essential that he equips himself with knowledge and skills imperative for a globalised economy in the 21st century. It is because of the foresight and vision of Prime Minister Jawahar Lal Nehru that apex institutes of higher learning and research in engineering and business management were established—Indian Institutes of Technology (IITs) and the Indian Institutes of Management (IIMs). These institutes—which are sometimes criticised for their elitist orientation are in the forefront of providing brain power for the corporate and information technology sectors in the country. True, quite a number of their students migrate to USA for better opportunities, but some of them do return to India and provide leadership to Indian enterprises. Those who criticise the misplaced emphasis of the Indian planning on expansion and strengthening of the tertiary education in the beginning, and consider higher education as 'non-merit good' (the current thinking in the UGC) tend to ignore the fact that in the absence of government investment in these institutions, the Indian students would not have been able to avail of the opportunities of upward mobility and excellence presently available to them. The infrastructure of higher education that India has been able to put in place in areas like biotechnology, information technology and applied sciences needs to be strengthened and improved.

India has a vast infrastructure of formal systems of education right from the primary and secondary level schools to colleges and universities at the tertiary levels. However, mention may be made of Navodaya Vidyalayas started in 1985-86 to provide good quality modern education to the talented children predominantly from the rural areas, Kendriya Vidyalayas for the children of the employees of public sector undertakings, central and state governments and those working in defence forces. The National Council of Educational Research and Training was established in 1961 with a view to ensuring qualitative improvement and excellence in school education as well as teachers education. It designs courses and generates software systems and also sets up resource centres for computer literacy in school projects.

The number of institutions imparting higher education numerically is impressive—214 universities including 16 central universities and 38 institutions declared deemed universities under the University Grants Commission Act, 1956. In terms of infrastructure and capability in the fields of teaching in medicine and research in agriculture, science and technology, the country has developed apex bodies including Indian Council of Medical Research (ICMR), Indian Council of Agricultural Research (ICAR) and Council of Scientific and Industrial Research (CSIR). The ICMR is entrusted with the responsibility to stop mushroom growth of medical colleges, besides maintenance of uniform standards of medical education; the ICAR promotes science and technology programmes in the areas of agricultural research, education and extension education. The ICAR research set up includes 45 central institutes, four national bureaux, 10 project directorates, 30 national research centres, 80 All India Coordinated Research Projects and four deemed Universities. The ICAR also promotes research, education and extension education through 28 state agricultural universities. The ICAR system is one of the largest such systems of highly trained and competent scientific manpower in the world. The CSIR, with its all-encompassing character has played crucial role in the transformation of several industrial sectors in the country and made wide ranging important contribution in the fields of drug and pharmaceuticals manufacture, agrochemicals, petroleum and petrochemicals and rural industries through its extensive network of 40 laboratories and 80 extension centres throughout the country.

India undoubtedly has an extensive-almost unwieldy set up of institutions of higher learning and research in most of the important disciplines; in some areas notable strides have indeed been made. It is a cliche to say that India has the third largest scientific manpower in the world. At the same time there is an utter dissatisfaction, by and large, at the quality of research and academic work being done. These institutions have become, in most of the cases large bureaucracies performing day-to-day maintenance functions.

The number of research papers published or abstracted by the Indian scientists in the international journals is not commensurate with the contribution expected of huge investment being made over the years. The academic and scientific institutions are fast becoming a pale shadow of huge government bureaucracies with senior scientists more interested in administrative work and responsibilities. In a leading agricultural university, a research editor—a senior scientist—entrusted with the task of editing scientific journals has been more interested in bringing out telephone and faculty directories, his own work remains in backlog for years, work which needs expertise of a scientist and a trained mind gets neglected and sidelined. A drastic improvement in the work culture of institutions of higher learning and research is generally called for but hardly implemented in actual practice.

Change is the defining concept, the term and the thought which depicts the tone and the temper of the contemporary society, and one of the major driving forces behind the change is the ever onward march of information technology. Information technology is fast becoming the nervous system of modern society, therefore in a changing world education is also changing fast.

The closing decade of the 20th century has witnessed the exponential growth in the ambit and application of communication technologies which have far reaching relevance to education, its expansion and quality. The implications of the growth in communication technologies impacting the very nature of learning process and education system, are equally far reaching, necessitating a continuous reassessment with respect to its effectiveness and scope. The traditional roles assigned to school, classroom and teacher and the expectation of the society in terms of quality of education are changing at a very fast pace. Concepts like the Learning Society, Interactive Technologies, Collaborative Learning, Knowledge Industries and Virtual University are not only transforming the way education is being imparted but is also changing the transmission of education itself.

New Information and Communication Technologies (NICTs) have brought human kind face-to-face with fundamental changes : by abolishing distances they are instrumental in shaping the societies of tomorrow; the most accurate, uptodate information (in fact information as the events are developing) is now available to anyone, anywhere in the world, often in real time and reaches the remotest regions.

Interactive media technologies make it possible not only to send and receive information, but to engage in dialogue, discussion and the transmission of information and knowledge, irrespective of distance or operating time. The harnessing of the potential of communication technologies for educational purposes—not in the restricted sense of structured formal academic system, but by way of opportunities for life long learning available throughout the life span of an individual, as well as of self-learning, has been another notable characteristic of the times which has brought about a conspicuous shift in the paradigm of education and learning.

As the world moves towards a knowledge-based, post-industrial information society, the crucial importance of education becomes self-evident. In the Indian situation stress would not only be to ensure basic education to every child, prevent dropouts and ensure relevance of education, but to also provide opportunities to those outside the conventional education system, and to the work force for continuing education. In developing countries there is growing awareness about the critical role of education : as also the conviction that since the traditional means of education suffer from several major deficiencies, these would not be able to cope with the challenges of emerging situation in the twenty-first century.

The dramatic emergence of information societies has led to a revolution in communications in the shape of multimedia systems and the spectacular expansion of information technology networks, including internet. Even though the impact of the expansion of internet is still limited in developing countries, owing to the relatively small number of people with the necessary technology know-how; every thing suggests that an unstoppable revolution is in progress which will make it possible to transmit an ever increasing mass of information in shorter span of time. At the same time, thanks to the falling cost of equipment, the new technologies are steadily finding their way into every aspect of work.

In his book, *The Death of Distance*, Frances Cairncross points out : The death of the distance as a determinant of the cost of communicating will probably be the single most important force shaping society in the first-half of the next century. Technological change has the power to revolutionize the way people live, and this one will be no exception. It will alter, in ways that are only dimly imaginable, decisions about where people work and what kind of work they do, concepts of national borders and sovereignty, and patterns of international trade. The death of distance will also give rise to proliferation of ideas. New ideas and information will travel faster to the remotest corner of the world. The Third World countries will have access to knowledge that the industrial world has long enjoyed.

Distance Education

At a time when knowledge industries are taking off at top speed, education has to be seen as a factor of crucial importance even as a part of economic policy. France has announced a new television channel known as 'knowledge channel'. This knowledge channel will work like the information highway—by extending its range and scope to benefit both the children and the adults.

The Report of International Commission on the Development of Education, 1972, *Learning to Be, The world of education—today and tomorrow*, articulated the concept of lifelong education as covering the entire educational process, from the point of view of the individual and of society. It first concerns the education of children and, while helping the child to live his own life as he deserves to do, its essential mission is to prepare the future adult for various forms of autonomy and self learning. This later learning requires many wide-ranging educational structures and cultural activities to be developed for adults. These, while existing for their own purpose, are also a pre-condition for reforming initial education. Another International Commission on Education for the Twenty-first Century, appointed by UNESCO in 1993, reaffirmed the concept of lifelong education. The title of the report, *Learning : The Treasure Within*, reminds us of the importance of learning throughout life, as also the need to develop an initiative and practice of education that goes beyond schooling. The treasure is learning itself—the remarkable asset possessed by every individual that needs to be harnessed and used wisely. Learning, knowledge and minds are not commodities to be developed and exploited, but treasures to be nurtured and cultivated to improve the quality of life—of the individuals as well as of the society. Learning throughout life will in due course become the heart beat of society.

A vast responsibility rests with the educational planners in formulating workable strategies towards providing educational opportunities for those who missed out in the first instance and also to reorient education to meet the demands of industry and economy. Since human knowledge is rapidly expanding in many fields, degrees gained years ago are no longer adequate qualifications. The introduction of new technologies, production methods and techniques advance more rapidly than the setting up of new specializations and new curricula at colleges, universities, and other academic and vocational education establishments. At the same time the rising aspirations for better quality of life have also induced several sections of society to pursue higher education.

It is obvious that the distance education and open learning institutes, which have come up in a big way, not only in the developed countries, but more so in the Third World countries could not have fulfilled the task of imparting education but for the use of communication technologies on a large scale. The role of the teacher—the key to the success of the educational system—also has to be changed; instead of dispensing information and knowledge he has to guide the students in the acquisition of knowledge from the ever expanding learning resources. The rapid development of communication in most countries, the expansion of various forms of mass communication and in particular of audiovisual communication, combined with the spread of informatics, open up new horizons and multiply the linkages between education and communication. There is an evident increase of the educational potential of communication. While the education system loses the monopoly of education, communication becomes itself a vehicle and subject for education.

As technology advances, the ideal of learning, "what you want, when you want, where you want, and at your own pace", becomes possible and lifelong learning is no longer just a slogan. A series of exciting new technological developments have significantly expanded and enhanced the instructional potential of television. Likewise computer technology has advanced at a remarkable pace, and should play a key role in the future educational expansion. The electronic media offers new dimensions to expand educational opportunities, to improve the quality of instruction, and to increase the cost effectiveness of the present educational system.

Tele-education, by all means, has been considered to be a landmark development. The extensive use of television for educational purposes in Asia in the two most populous countries of the region—China and India, the limitations of being one way medium notwithstanding, is indicated by two important developments : The largest distance reaching institution of the world, the national multimedia distance learning institution in China, is called the Central Radio and Television University (CRTVU), and one of the largest communications experiments in which television programmes were received by local viewers directly from space—Satellite Instructional Television Experiment (SITE) was conducted in India for a period of one year from 1 August 1975.

While the SITE has been extensively documented in the communication literature, the contribution of CRTVU needs to be highlighted in the context of the role of open learning system. The CRTVU employs broadcast as the main delivery vehicle and supplements it with print, audio visual media, tutorials and computerized instruction. Programmes are broadcast directly to learners at home, in the workplace or the study centres located throughout the country. The CRTVU courses follow a multi-media approach. The input of non-print media varies according to the subject area—science and engineering courses have greater proportion of TV programmes, whereas radio is the chief medium for social science courses. TV programmes are transmitted by the Central China Television (CCTV) nationally through the microwave network.

The remarkable aspect of the working of CRTVU is the expansion of its operations in rural areas to meet the shortages of technically trained manpower. The university has been able to create a vast network to meet the shortage of educated persons in various fields and also the demands of fresh graduates from high schools, since it is not possible for the provincial universities to meet these demands.

In a country like Pakistan, where most of the population is illiterate, the role of television as an educational institution is of real importance. The Pakistan TV made substantial contribution to adult education; adult education programmes were broadcast regularly and adult education centres were established in rural areas equipped with television sets. Its instructional programmes, which include physical education, calligraphy, fine art, legal consultation and education about traffic rules are transmitted regularly. It also includes various programmes to boost civic sense and lectures on different courses taught at Allama Iqbal Open University have been a regular feature of education programming.

The rapid expansion of television in India during 1984, facilitated the launching of the countrywide classroom (CWCR) project by the University Grants Commission. The programme is aimed primarily for the undergraduate students of colleges located at different places. The contents of CWCR programmes are not linked to any examination, these are neither based on a particular syllabus. Instead these telecasts seek to provide new insights, bring new findings and take the students to various places and laboratories they would rarely see. The project aims at the widest possible utilisation of television's potential to improve the quality of university level education.

Another important form of technology being widely used in distance education is teleconferencing. Teleconferencing is an interactive electronic communication among two or more locations. The attraction for adopting teleconferencing is said to be the savings it results in minimizing physical travel. The time saving involved in this process is also a significant factor and the experience of advanced countries in which teleconferencing is in wide usage shows that apart from economy and time saving, this technology improves corporate efficiency and enables participatory management.

The World Bank, in its World Development Report, 1998-99, *Knowledge for Development* points out as to how expanding telecommunications hold the promise to improve every developing country's capacity to absorb knowledge by providing opportunities for high quality, low cost adult learning. The Virtual University of the Monterrey Institute of Technology in Mexico is a consortium of collaborating universities including 13 outside the country. It enrolls 9,000 degree and 35,000 nondegree students each year in Mexico and other Latin American countries. It delivers courses through printed texts and live and pre-recorded television broadcasts, with communication between students and faculty aided by computers and the Internet.

The African Virtual University, headquartered in Nairobi, seeks to increase University enrolments and improve the quality and relevance of instruction in business, science, and engineering throughout Africa. In each participating country, a local institution is competitively selected to oversee operations. This institution provides hardware and software for interactive courses, registers students, supervises study programmes, offers a structured study environment, and awards local course credit. The University has installed 27 satellite receiver terminals throughout Africa and developed a digital library, to compensate for the dearth of scientific journals in African Universities. Although it is too early to assess results, such initiatives give reason to hope that new technology can make a big contribution to narrowing knowledge gaps.

A virtual classroom comprises electronic classroom from which the class is taught, a network of specially equipped electronic classrooms at which the students are present, and the satellite, microwave or cable linkages between them. For teaching purposes, virtual classrooms can either be two-way video with two-way audio, often called video conferencing or more accurately video teaching or one-way video and two-way audio.

The learning technologies offer valuable opportunities to expand educational infrastructure to improve the quality of instruction, and to increase the cost-effectiveness of present education systems. However, they also can become educational "white elephants" that consume a nation's financial resources without effectively delivering the much needed instruction that was originally hoped for. Media projects, with their heavy initial start-up costs, represent an especially unnerving, educational gamble for developing nations. While their potential to reach large numbers of students may be tremendous, if that potential is not realized, the financial losses can be staggering, especially for an already impoverished country. The implementation of large educational media projects is generally very complicated, and the possibility exists for major difficulties arising in different ways (*Educational Media in Retrospect, Discussion Paper—Education and Training Series, the World Bank 1987*).

The unique potential of electronic media to transcend barriers create logistical challenges. The modern electronic media are seen as a means to overcome vast distances, overcoming topography, and underdeveloped communications infrastructures. So, educational media projects are designed for some of the least accessible regions. It is no wonder that some of these projects fall short of expectations, when they are carried out in the hope that they may transcend adverse circumstances that cannot be overcome in any other way. Another managerial challenge is the difficulty of overseeing such a complex range of projects, which include procuring equipment, hiring personnel, producing programmes, distributing written material, dealing with international agencies, etc. To further complicate matters, many of these activities involve a high degree of technical expertise, so that various specialists must be brought into the project. Administrators sometimes do not fully understand the needs of these technicians.

In most of the Asian countries access to personal computers, modem, and domestic TV, telephone and VCR for the learners may not be feasible for years to come. Therefore, creating a Virtual University in the Asian context would continue to be a vision for a large number of Asian countries. Technologies such as audio cassettee players, television and VCR, even though familiar to the students, constitute essentially leisure and entertainment media and till such time as sustained efforts are made to reorient these technologies for instructional purposes their potential may not be fully utilised.

A caveat needs to be entered regarding over-optimism of the effectiveness of the educational technologies in certain situations. Educational television, for instance suffers from certain limitations, the most serious being the element of anonymity inherent in its very operation. It is strictly a one-way communication. The teacher-taught contact, considered vital all over the world, is almost missing in the case of television—no physical contact, no physical identification, no scope for repetition, clarification or elaboration.

The hype about NICTs apart (industry as well as the corporate sectors are quite upbeat about information technology) it is difficult to visualise a situation when the school as an institution, school teacher, the black board and traditional person-to-person instructional methods will fade away. The need for school organization, for teachers as dispensers of knowledge and not merely as managers and organisers of resource centres, will continue to be felt, regardless of NICT's potential. In this context it is relevant to take note of what the Human Development in South Asia 1998 says : Another notable example of distance education comes from within South Asia itself. Allama Iqbal Open University in Pakistan has successfully employed interactive radio for many of its education programmes. A recent survey revealed that rural participation in distance learning programmes was much higher than urban, and that female participation was as high as 32 per cent. The overall assessment is that while distance education can help, and while mass media can play an important role in the new information age which we are entering, there is still no substitute for regular schooling—formal or non-formal. After all a school is not just a concrete structure. It is a meeting place for children where they form lifelong friendships, where their character is moulded by their teachers, where discipline is learned; where learning to be responsible citizens through tolerant interactions in a society is as essential a lesson as any reading or writing skill.

India has made rapid headway in imparting education through distance education mode and open learning system both at the school and tertiary level. The open learning system has brought about a virtual revolution in education—in terms of the number of institutions offering education through the above mode, the number of students who join courses offered by these institutions, the new programmes of study introduced and multi-media usage employed in this mode of education. Heralding the revolution are two institutions at the national level—Indira Gandhi National Open University (IGNOU) established in 1985 and the National Open School (NOS) set up in 1989. There are of course eight other open universities in the country; numerous universities also offer a number of courses through their directorates of distance education.

The IGNOU which provides higher education in the country through multi-media distance education mode is patterned on the British Open University. Compared to traditional Indian Universities, IGNOU's admission procedures and academic programmes are more flexible. The major objectives of the University include widening access to higher education to larger segments of population, organising programmes of continuing education and initiating programmes of higher education for specific target groups like women, people living in backward regions, hilly areas, etc. The University has innovated multi-media instructional strategy comprising printed material, audio visual aids, supported by counselling sessions at a network of study centres throughout the country. It has so far launched 39 programmes comprising 486 courses. During 1997 over 1.63 lakh students were registered for various programmes of study. Since 1998 the University has made phenomenal progress in introducing latest information technologies—teleconferencing, phone-in radio programmes, etc. It has also widened the base of its programmes by introducing computer education in a large number of centres throughout the country.

The National Open School, a pioneering institute of open learning at school level, serves an equally important purpose of making education accessible to the marginalised groups—rural youth, scheduled castes and scheduled tribes, ex-servicemen and the handicapped. The NOS mission statement includes universalisation of education, enhancing social equity and creating a learning society as its objectives. Established in 1989, the NOS provides education to school dropouts and those who cannot attend regular classes. It offers basic, secondary, senior secondary, vocational education and life enrichment programmes. Noteworthy aspects of its working are : (1) By making use of the existing school network to serve its students, it benefits from that infrastructure while at the same time enriching it by bringing in facilities not normally available to the schools, (2) Use of more advanced technologies such as instructional television, audio and video programmes for the enrichment of courses in addition to face-to-face contact with the students, and (3) Greater flexibility and freedom to choose from a combination of vocational and academic courses—offered in English and a number of local languages.

Technological innovations open up vast new possibilities. However, a world of caution is necessary: they are not instant miracles, but tools to be introduced and used only after careful consideration is given to all possible resulting ramifications. Each has particular potential, yet none is an isolated means; they are parts of a total system, which should be planned and shaped bearing in mind the integration of all its parts. Technological innovations can often have negative effects, both economic and social, and may distort directions and priorities for overall development activities. However, inviting introduction of some new technologies is often easier than subsequent provision of software required for their optimum utilization. This has been repeatedly brought home to the educational planners and administrators in developing countries; but implementation of this advice is always tardy.

In a paper, *Application of Interactive Technologies in Open and Distance Learning : An overview*, AW Khan and Patricia McWillams, detail comprehensively barriers to the use and expansion of educational technology in a significant way. The authors have articulated the dilemma, frequently mentioned in the context of the limitations to the applications of educational technology in distance education programmes : It would be remiss not to recognise the present lack of available technical infrastructure of sufficient quality to support distance education on a wide-spread basis in many countries and regions of the world. Although here too one can be optimistic given the speed of growth and penetration in this sector we are still, in many instances, dealing with 'dirt roads in the age of the 'information highway' and we are driving on that road with tractors, not high performance sports cars of the 90s. In practical terms, it is extremely difficult to effectively deliver quality education using an audio-conferencing system when half of the receive sites are off-line due to technical difficulties at the local telco! A further important component to an efficient technical infrastructure is experienced and trained human resources, a commodity which often requires several years to develop adequately.

NICTs and more conventional multi-media, are all too often perceived as panaceas, that can bring about revolutionary educational change and immediate progress in developing countries. If care is not taken, the developing world is likely to be strewn with the sad remains of highly expensive communications equipments, unused and unloved as far as teachers and students are concerned; in all such cases success depends upon ensuring that media technology fulfils the needs of learners, teachers, employers and the society.

REFERENCES

Dreze, Jean and Sen, Amartya (1995). *India : Economic Development and Social Opportunity*. Oxford University Press, Delhi.

Frances Cairncross (1997). *The Death of Distance*. Harvard Business School Press. Boston Massachusetts.

Haq, Mahbub ul (1998). *Human Development in South Asia 1998*. Oxford University Press, Karachi.

Human Development Report (1996). UNDP. Oxford University Press, Oxford.

India (1999). A Reference Annual. Publications Division, New Delhi.

Indian Journal of Adult Education (1985). New Delhi.

Report of International Commission on Education for 21st Century (1996). *Learning, The Treasure Within*. UNESCO, Paris.

Schramm. Wilbur (1964). *Mass Media and National Development.* The Role of Information in the Developing Countries. Stanford University Press and UNESCO, Paris.

Tahir. Seemi Naghmana (1996). Television in Pakistan—An Overview. In : *Contemporary Television—Eastern Perspectives.* French David and Richards Michael (eds.) Sage Publications, New Delhi.

UNESCO (1972). *Learning to Be The World of* Education. Today and Tomorrow. Paris.

The World Bank (1998-99). World Development Report, *Knowledge for Development.* Washington. D. C., U. S. A.

NOTE

Since NICTs are being extensively used for educational and learning purposes; in several countries technology based education is developing into online instruction; and the terms being used are not only Learning Technologies but also New Learning Technologies (see Mirza J.S., *IJOL, 7(1), 98; pp.89*) these terms are being used interchangeably.

5

Communication for Rural Development

Ever since the beginning of economic planning, rural development has received an overriding priority. That is as it should be, because it was Mahatama Gandhi who said : Village development is the key to India's development. Rapid expansion of urban population notwithstanding, a massive 629 million people (74.3 per cent of total population) constitute the rural population. Since the development of rural areas in terms of infrastructure, education and health care facilities had remained severely neglected for a number of years, it was therefore logical that planning should address the needs of rural areas urgently.

The Eighth Five Year Plan gives a comprehensive definition of rural development : Rural Development implies both the economic development of people as well as greater social transformation. Increased participation of the people in the rural development process, decentralisation of planning, better enforcement of land reforms and greater access to credit with better prospects for economic development. Improvement in health, education, drinking water, energy supply, sanitation and housing coupled with attitudinal changes also facilitates their social development.

Inspite of massive investments in the rural development and poverty alleviation programmes the benefits have not percolated down to the poor and the intended beneficiaries.

Several factors have been responsible for such a situation: the existing power structure of village institutions such as panchayats and cooperative societies which are captured by the rich and the politically influential people; centralised planning process emanating from the union government and lack of awareness about the development programmes and projects available. It is now being increasingly realised that although we have a functioning democratic government in our country, people have hardly any role in shaping their destinies at various levels which has severely affected the quality of governance in the country. The planning is mostly Delhi-centric; and the planning process concentrated in the offices of the central government and the planning commission. There have not been many people sponsored and village sponsored schemes.

There has been repeated criticism of the whole concept of development and the way the task of planned development was initiated and implemented. There has been greater realization that the economic betterment of the poor sections cannot be achieved without social transformation involving structural changes, educational development, growth in awareness, and change in outlook, motivation and attitudes. Social change can be achieved through greater participation of the poor by electing them to the grass-root level institutions. The Seventh Five Year Plan (1985-90) document says : Improvement of literacy and education, both through formal and non-formal means, and the imaginative use of the mass media for communicating useful information and knowledge as well as for changing the outlook of the people by instilling in them the egalitarian spirit, the urge for and confidence in achieving self betterment through cooperative endeavour, are essential for setting up the process of socio-economic transformation. It is now being frequently admitted that due to deficiencies noticed in the implementation of plan projects, illiteracy and lack of awareness on the part of beneficiaries, and chain of intermediaries, on the other hand, only a small portion of the intended outlay reaches the actual recipients.

Another serious drawback with our planning efforts is the centralised planning and approach to development. The history of country's development planning shows that all measures to tackle poverty, generate employment and promote a more equitable socio-economic order through different programmes like Integrated Rural Development Programme (IRDP), Jawahar Rozgar Yojna (JRY), Drought Prone Areas Programmes (DPAP), Small Farmers Development Agency (SFDA) have emanated from the centre. Several of the state governments have not been very enthusiastic about these programmes.

What ails our planning philosophy would be clear from the two instances being quoted from the proceedings of the D.T. Lakdawala Memorial Symposium lectures organised in 1993 :

1. Pointing to the dichotomy prevailing in the development process, George Fernandes highlighted the mind set that guides our administration regarding big projects vs small projects and bisleri culture vs plain drinking water. He said : "Take big projects like Narmada and Tehri. You bring money from foreign countries for constructing these big dams. Many people are displaced, they lose their land, their forest and all sources of their livelihood. They get completely ruined. So, while on one hand, we construct big dams, choose the path of development based on large scale industrialization, in the same breath, we talk of decentralisation. Again the contradictions involved in such an approach are ignored. A new thinking is needed, a holistic approach is necessary to build a new India, a better India, a just India". Fernandes said : The more I think on this, the more worried I become, because I am witness to how we all have become slaves of a particular civilization. I am happy that today, here, we have been served plain water. Now-a-days in ministerial and official meetings, mineral water, Bisleri, is served. Even if you go to the residence of political leaders you are not served plain water. The gap between ordinary people and leadership has become enormously wide due to the kind of planning we have pursued during the last 45 years. The end result of this is that the policy-makers themselves

have become aware that water supplied to ordinary people is not potable. And that is why the planners and the executors of those plans, the politicians, and administrators keep mineral water, Bisleri, costing ten to twelve rupees—I do not know the exact price—a bottle, in their homes. They know that water supplied through the local bodies is not pure. Without even a modicum of protest we have accepted that the tap water we get is not potable, that it is in fact dangerous to drink the water we get from our taps. If there is a sharp variation between our goals and the present development model and the culture it has generated, we cannot ignore it. If we do not understand this contradiction I am of the view that nothing substantial will result from whatever we may resolve.

2. Participating in the same symposium, the Deputy Chairman of the Planning Commission, Pranab Mukherjee observed : Recently, I was going through the district planning documents of particular district and I found that to implement a developmental outlay of Rs. 8 crores in a year, the actual establishment cost is more than Rs. 16 crores. What type of planning is possible in such a situation? And in certain areas, I noticed, in that district, at the village level, at the lowest level, there are as many as 26 functionaries either fully or partly belonging to both sets of governments, state and central. And none of them are fully engaged. Now how to coordinate these things and have an integrated approach. And if we had that, perhaps with much less cost we could have achieved much more. So, decentralisation of planning, to my mind, is not merely a cliche or slogan, it is an urgent necessity. From our experiences we have found that we cannot achieve some of our targets in the areas of afforestation, literacy and population control. The involvement of people is the key to the success of these programmes. And surely, the involvement of the people is not possible through the bureaucratic apparatus.

Unless we can convert the slogan of literacy into some sort of mass movement, mass participation, nothing is going to help us. Today in some of the districts that are declaring themselves totally literate, mass participation and mass involvement is there in a big way, and without mass involvement, total literacy could not have been achieved.

The opinions expressed at the seminar circuits generally do not travel beyond the precints of the seminar halls and remain useful as quotable quotes, but I do see that things are beginning to change; the perceptions about the small dams and big dams at the World Bank level are changing and as literacy increases, the development bureaucracy is bound to become more accountable.

Another fashionable thing is to speak in the name of the common people; however now it is becoming increasingly clear that common people are now becoming more and more demanding and assertive as to why their elected representatives are not delivering. The recent elections to the Parliament have sent a message to the elected representatives of the people—loud and clear—deliver or forfeit the trust of the electorate. It was perhaps the first election ever where development became the central theme. Perhaps there may not be turning back now.

It is not the objective of this paper to run down every aspect of the planning process in the country, but the fact remains that one of our former Prime Ministers had gone on record saying that out of every rupee that the Centre spends on each of these schemes, only 20 paise reaches the targeted beneficiary. P. Sainath, the well known journalist who has made significant contribution to our understanding of rural poverty and whose book, *Everybody Loves a Good Drought, Stories from India's Poorest Districts*, gives a graphic account of rampant corruption prevailing at the grassroot level of development bureaucracy. He refers to one such instance, which is better reproduced in his own words :

> A corrupt Block Development Officer (BDO) came. And what he said you cannot hear that even in a Bollywood film. He was asking for bribes from a few young people. He takes 25 per cent. If the work to be done in your village costs Rs. 10,000, then he should be given Rs. 2,500. This is the rate, it

> has to be given. He went to one village, Eshak village, a communist village. There was a young boy. He became emotional, it was the question of his pride, self-respect. Next day they came to the BDO's office and called him out. He had demanded 25 per cent, isn't it? Twenty-five young men came there and beat him 25 times with their chappals. Then the BDO filed a case of dacoity, brigandry, murder, etc., against these boys. When the case was in the process, I was there. The BDO was telling them, "I am willing to drop the cases, I bear you no grudge", he is a businessman. He was telling the leader of the group, "*are yarr, sir ko mara, dil ko mara, izzat ko mara arre hai pet me math maro*, give me my 25 per cent, I will do your work and withdraw my case against you, I have got my transfer already." These kinds of negotiations were going on in the court right in front of everybody.[1]

It is only to curb the rampant corruption in rural development works that the campaign for Right to Information has been gathering strength in several states in the country. In Rajasthan the campaign has metamorphosed into a movement from grassroots embedded in the protest by villagers in several districts. The movement essentially aims at ensuring accountability in development projects. The campaign, which was basically to obtain photocopies of bills, receipts, muster rolls and other documents concerning project accounts got its inspiration from several *Jan sunwayis* (open public hearings) organised by the Mazdoor, Kisan Shakti Sangathan (MKSS) where hundreds of the poorest from far off villages came to speak, listen and share their experiences. Since the bureaucracy found such a movement challenging its authority, a stalemate ensued in getting any access to information legislation through.

1. Exploring the Heartland—An Agenda for the media.

The Prime Minister's recent assurance that government was working on the right to information law so as to make information more accessible to people has once again given hope that accountability in the execution of development projects would be ensured, and to that extent quality maintained. The Prime Minister said : Once this law is in position, media would stand to gain tremendously in its efforts to keep the people informed. This crucial step—never a day too soon—would go a long way in enabling media to play a catalytic role in rural development.

Commenting on this aspect of rural development schemes, the well-known social activist Bunker Roy says : Because the system is so corrupt, because there is no accountability and no fear of being caught and suspended, every year millions of rupees of funds earmarked for building schools, dispensaries, houses, drinking water schemes, planting sapling in forest land, and construction of dams, community centres, go into the pockets of gram sewaks (village workers), *patwaris* and village level officials in league with touts and politicians. This is the situation in all the South Asian region, without exception, where the governments have taken the responsibility to deliver development schemes to the poor in villages.[2]

The enthusiasm generated by the campaign and the spontaneous response it has elicited reminds me of an other similar movement—*Chipko*. There is a definite need for several more such initiatives which would change the face of rural India. The initiative taken by the National Institute of Rural Development, Hyderabad in September 1997 in organising a national workshop on right to information was a significant milestone in the campaign for people's right to information.

The draft of the model bill, finalised at the Hyderabad workshop in 1997, suggested amendments to the earlier draft bill of the Press Council of India. Such a step is bound to have long term impact on how rural development plans are executed in the country. *The draft is being included as an annexure to the chapter* (pp. 115-124).

2. The Public and the Patwari in HIMAL, South Asia, May-June 1997.

Communication Strategies for Rural Development

Rural development strategies followed by India and other countries laid emphasis on economic growth in the form of more production, increase in income and employment generating activities, the basic objective being fulfilling basic needs and alleviation of rural poverty. Since most of the developing countries are agrarian economies, agricultural development naturally received the highest priority. It was generally accepted that agricultural development through the introduction to technology could contribute to the overall economic development. This thinking led to the introduction of new technology in agriculture.

The strategy adopted for agricultural development has been multi-dimensional and broad-based : Center-to-village level administrative machinery to implement development programmes; large scale production of chemical fertilizers and, of course, the nationwide network of agricultural research, extension and education facilities.

India has one of the largest systems of agricultural research and education in the world; apex institute being the Indian Council of Agricultural Research (ICAR). The state agricultural universities (SAUs) in the country and the regional research stations, based on agroclimatic zones carry out research on evolution of improved varieties, disease and pest control measures and fertilizer application, etc. Several universities have fairly well developed departments of extension education—both in agriculture and home sciences; and communication centres which bring out extension, research and academic publications and conduct kisan melas and training programmes for the farmers. Since the productivity levels in agriculture depend to a large extent, on the response a farmer gives to the various strategies of agricultural development, all efforts are geared to reach the farmers through all forms of media-interpersonal (farmer's fairs, meetings and visits), print and electronic media (rural press, farm and home programmes from All India Radio and Krishi Darshan Programme on Television). The author has been intimately associated with planning and guiding some of these programmes—first as the head of Farm and Information and Communication Service (FICS), and subsequently as Course Director of the agricultural journalism programme for scientists and development workers from the agricultural universities and development departments from all over the country. The section on communication strategies, derives its recommendations from the findings of research projects in the agricultural journalism course apart from a discussion on the role of print media in agricultural development.

The Indian press—by far the freest press in South Asia, pluralistic, multi-lingual, continues to be largely urban-oriented. More so the metropolitan press; and the newspapers coming out from the national capital are Delhi centric. The press in English language is elitist, geared to the commercial culture, obsessed with garnering the maximum share of advertising revenue. Issues concerning rural development are not given adequate coverage. In a study concerning content analysis of coverage of agricultural and rural development issues in four newspapers in English language, the researcher A. K. Singh concluded that small coverage given to these issues was due to the fact these newspapers do not have substantial circulation in the rural areas and the professional interests of the newspapers are not served in any way by giving such news. The content analysis which included four newspapers—*The Hindu*, *Times of India*, *Hindustan Times* and the *Indian Express* for forty-two days between January-June 1996 found that most of the contents of agricultural and rural development reporting were related to economic aspects rather than the ones relating to agricultural research and problems of agriculture. *The Hindu* was the only newspaper which regularly gave weekly page on various aspects of agriculture including the latest information in the field of research.

Reporting agricultural and rural issues is constrained by several factors : According to popular perceptions, rural development reporting is not considered glamorous or prestigious enough; in the reporter's scale of prestige, rural reporting occupies a low rung. Every young reporter dreams of covering politics, defence or foreign policy, rather than specialising in rural, agricultural development reporting. Rural sector is so diffused and variegated including agricultural policies and operations, cooperatives, changing village milieu—that it cannot be packaged into a neat, well defined slot. These and other constraints have relegated rural reporting to a back slot in an otherwise expanding media landscape in the country.

Notwithstanding the above constraints there have been some outstanding examples of reporting rural development by leading newspapers in Kerala, specially *Malayala Manorama*, *Mathrubhoomi*, *Kerala Kaumudi* and *Desabhimani*. These newspapers have weekly farm feature pages which include articles, news stories, success stories of farmers, etc. with pictures. Some of these newspapers have taken to organising kisan melas and farmers' meets—functions which are generally performed by agricultural universities and research institutes. These farmers' meets afford a valuable opportunity to farmers and farm experts to exchange information and views on various aspects of agriculture and associated areas. *Malayala Manorama* honours the best farmer of Kerala once in two years by awarding the title *Karshaka Sri*, a citation and Rs. 1 lakh. The panel of judges for the selection is led by two of world's most outstanding farm experts, Dr. M. S. Swaminathan and V. Kurien, both World Food Prize winners. The contribution made by the Malayalam press to agricultural development has been highlighted in an article by R. Hali in a special issue of *Kurukshetra* devoted to Media and Rural India. Hali concludes his article by saying : The Malayalam dailies have created a golden chapter in the history of creative development journalism by introducing the weekly farm feature page and running it for the last twenty years. Now every year, nearly 100 million pages are made available for farm news by the Malayalam dailies. They have really set, a creative replicable model to the nation and to the developing countries.

Radio—Tool for Rural Development

As a tool for development communication, reaching out to the people with relevant messages and usable information, and to encourage people's participation in the 'Open Forum' which it eventually provides, Community Radio is the ideal medium.

It is interesting to note that several recent studies undertaken on media-related issues, clearly prove that, contrary to popular impression about marginalisation of radio, it continues to serve the village community effectively through its farm broadcasts. From the number of radio sets available and in use by the farmers in rural areas and the frequency and variety of programmes related to agriculture and rural development, including programmes like Farm Radio School, it is apparent that radio still enjoys primary importance in disseminating message of rural development. The policy makers and planners, in both the sectors—development as well as information and communication—need to re-order their priorities and densify radio broadcasting—in terms of number of radio stations, availability of cheap radio sets and larger budgetary allocation for staff recruitment and upgradation of their knowledge and skills. The continued step motherly treatment meted out to radio broadcasting signifies a particular mind set of policy planners which is conditioned more by glamour and hightech hype rather than the hard realities of human condition of the rural poor and the marginalised sections of the Indian society.

That the Indian television has become primarily a medium for family entertainment and development programmes do not enjoy a large viewership has also been highlighted by a Doordarshan study. The study conducted by the Audience Research Unit of Doordarshan during January-March 1993, covering 420 villages from 15 states, observed that though Doordarshan entertainment programmes have a large viewership in villages, the development oriented programmes do not enjoy the same popularity. Some of the other findings of the study are :

1. Regional programmes are assumed to serve a very large area. Yet the programmes of Bangalore Kendra

may not be relevant to the people in the northern districts of Karnataka. This lack of local specificity and context has a bearing on the viewership. The Doordarshan development programmes have, therefore, not been as effective as they should have been.

2. A total viewership of any programme is dependent not only on the rating, but also on the number of persons viewing from a set. A common observation is that in villages, domestic sets often become community sets, attracting people from other households.

This study also collected information about the average number of persons watching a particular programme from one set, whereas nine viewers watched film-based programmes, only two opted for the programmes on agriculture.

Demystifying the Media Profession

Knowledge, understanding and expertise in communication practice and profession should not be the exclusive prerogative of the media professionals. This need to be extended through a basic training course to all experts and workers at various levels working in the areas of rural development, health, sanitation and other nation-building activities. A basic appreciation of the elements of communication needs to be imparted through appropriate short term courses. Media specialists, sociologists and development planners should work out inter-disciplinary mechanism for identifying the audience requirement, establishing proper feedback systems and extend guidance in the evaluation of effectiveness of communication programmes.

Radio and TV broadcasting, essentially a part of mass media communication process, share the characteristics and limitations of such a system. In such a system amount of feedback readily available is low, the message flow tends to be one-way and can be used to increase knowledge. Interpersonal medium, on the other hand, tends to be two-way, the amount of feedback readily available is high and is best used in situations calling for attitude formation and change.

Interpersonal medium, which in the context of rural development would include extension workers in the agriculture and community development departments of the state governments, personnel of agricultural agencies like MFALA and agro-industries centres and extension setup of agricultural universities and research institutes, would provide necessary reinforcement and supplement media programmes. Coordination between extension agencies and rural broadcasting will make these programmes more purposive and meaningful.

A noteworthy initiative in crystallising interest in the conditions of the rural poor and marginalised sections of society from all over the country has recently been taken by the Press Institute of India by launching the monthly journal in English and Hindi—*Grassroots*. Expressing the rationale of taking up the initiative, the doyen of the Indian journalists and the Director, Press Institute of India, Ajit Bhattacharjea says : The overall picture projected by the national press is ugly. It portrays an acquisitive, conflict ridden, middle class society, eager to achieve western standards of affluence, but unconcerned with the condition of human infrastructure at its base. And so we find nothing in the papers about panchayats, and empowerment, agriculture and the rural economy, literacy, unemployment, social tension. Yet without such coverage, the press fails its democratic function of monitoring the condition of society as a whole. It cannot claim the status of the Fourth Estate.

The *Grassroots* brings to its readers the news stories from Andhra villagers in search of drinking water, right to information campaign in Rajasthan and the success stories of NGOs. The August 1999 issue highlights the exploitation of Orissa tribals for bauxite (the adverse impact on the local population of alumina and bauxite mining projects located on tribal land in the Rayagada) and the November issue announces award for best feature to Richard Mahapatra on villagers protecting forests in Orissa.

India—with its vast population of 1 billion people—with seventy per cent living in rural areas— severely need more such initiatives. Let it not be said of its planners, writers and communication experts that they showed no propensity to solve the problems such as alleviation of poverty, illiteracy and lack of guidance and sharing of development experience with other sections of society to make development an all-encompassing and participatory process.

RESEARCH SUMMARIES IN AGRICULTURAL INFORMATION

The premier organisation conducting research in agriculture, Indian Agricultural Research Institute (IARI), had emphasised that agricultural universities and extension departments organise short term courses for agricultural scientists to train them in writing technical articles in simple language by using local equivalents for technical terms. To gear the scientists to the task of writing for farmers is a difficult proposition, mainly because of their preference for research paper writing. In pursuance of the above recommendations, the author in 1996 conceived and directed a Post-Graduate Diploma Course in Agricultural Journalism at Haryana Agricultural University. The programme has been developed to achieve the following objectives : To acquaint the participants with the role and principles of agricultural journalism and development communication; familiarise them with the process involved in print and electronic media; expose them to practical skills in writing for farmers and farm families, research publications, feature writing and newspapers and preparing radio and television programmes; and to sensitise them to various tasks and skills in public relations and public service campaigns.

Since 1996, agricultural scientists and development workers from all over the country including Karnataka, Andaman and Nicobar Islands, Tamil Nadu and Rajasthan, have undergone training. As an essential part of the programme, the trainees take up a research project as one of the information/communication aspects of agriculture. Some of the subjects have been : Effectiveness of Farm and Home Units Programmes of All India Radio; TV Viewing behaviour, Critical analysis of agricultural news reporting in leading newspapers, and many more on allied subjects. Research studies undertaken by the participants have been summarised. These studies analyse the effectiveness of sources of farm information and provide useful insight into the communication experiences.

1. Effectiveness of Farm and Home Unit's Programme of All India Radio, Delhi

Jai Parkash Singh Dabas (1998)

In order to achieve the target of increased food production so as to meet the needs of ever increasing population, the scientists need to develop appropriate technologies, which are environment friendly, within the reach of the farmers and contribute to sustainable agricultural production. The generation of technology alone will not help achieve the target, but we have to devise effective strategy for regular and quick transfer of these technologies to the ultimate users—the farmers for adoption. In country like ours, majority of the farmers are resource poor, illiterate having diversified needs, speaking different dialects, with poor telecommunication and electricity facilities in the villages. In such a situation radio is the cheapest, most convenient and important medium for educating the rural folk about latest agricultural technologies through quick communication, regardless of the distance and literacy level. The present national coverage of All India Radio is 90.6 per cent by area and 97.3 per cent by population (*Manorama Year Book*, 1996). The country has a network of about 185 radio stations, broadcasting rural programmes on different topics, in different languages and as per the agro-eco-requirement of their range. In order to ensure effective transfer of technical know-how in its intended form to the farmers, coverage alone is not important, but the content of programme should be relevant and informative in terms of farmer's need, and timing and mode of presentation should be effective. The Delhi station of All India Radio caters to the needs of the farmers of Delhi villages, Faridabad and Gurgaon districts of Haryana,

Ghaziabad, Meerut, Saharanpur, Muzaffarnagar, Bulandshahar and Aligarh districts of western Uttar Pradesh. Farmers from Rohtak, Sonepat, Panipat and Karnal districts also listen to the AIR Delhi programmes. The Farm and Home Unit of AIR, Delhi has three important programmes exclusively for agricultural development : *Krishi Charcha* at 6.55 a.m. (5 minutes), *Unnat Krishi* at 2.10 p.m. (10 minutes) and *Krishi Jagat* at 7.05 p.m. (25 minutes).

The objectives of the study were : To study the effectiveness of the content and timeliness of the programmes, and also the mode of presentation adopted in these programmes. The study was conducted for the programmes broadcast by Farm and Home Unit of All India Radio, Delhi station during June 1998. The broadcasts were categorised under 15 sub-heads for making quantitative evaluation of the programmes. Response from 30 farmers from two villages (15 from each village) Palla and Akbarpur Majra was received; information so collected was tabulated and analysed for drawing logical conclusions.

The *Krishi Charcha* programme is prepared and broadcast by the staff of Farm and Home Unit, and the mode of presentation is talk. *Unnat Krishi* programme is broadcast by recording it in advance and is presented by experts, the mode of presentation is talk. *Krishi Jagat*, which is the oldest programme broadcasts information under five sub-heads : News from agricultural commodity markets, scientific information on any topic of agriculture, *lok geet*, weather forecast and news, next day's programmes.

The study is confined to the second component i.e. scientific information on any topic from agriculture which is selected as per farmers need during that period. Time devoted to this part is 10 minutes. The information is presented by following interview mode of presentation or discussion. The interview is between expert invited from Agril. Research system or administration and staff of AIR. Sometimes a farmer is also invited and then mode of presentation is discussion between these three.

Under the *Krishi Charcha* programme the broadcast topics have been categorised into 15 major groups for analysis purposes. The data revealed that 23.1 per cent time was devoted to agronomy, followed by plant protection (19.8%), soil and fertilizer management (16.5%), vegetable (13.2%) and orchards (9.9%). Animal Husbandry ranked at sixth place having 6.6 per cent of the total time share.

Broadcast data for *Unnat Krishi* programme indicate that maximum broadcast time was devoted to agronomy (19.8%) followed by orchards (13.2%). About one-third time was devoted to these two topics. Vegetables and plant protection were given 10 per cent time each of the total broadcast; other categories covered in the broadcast were rainfed agriculture (6.6%), weed management (3.3%), animal husbandry (3.3%), poultry (3.3%), fisheries (3.3%), piggery and goatry (3.3%), agricultural engineering (3.3%) but their share was quite poor. Mushroom cultivation and floriculture were again completely ignored, although these are two important emerging aspects on which no information was provided to the farmers.

Krishi Jagat is the oldest and popular programme broadcast in the evening. In this programme also agronomy got the major share of the broadcast (23.3%) followed by soil and fertilizer management (16.6%). Agronomy alongwith soil and fertilizer management constitutes the major portion of the broadcast i.e. about 40 per cent. Plant protection got 10 per cent share and ranks third in broadcast priority. Vegetables and animal husbandry were devoted 6.6 per cent time each. Some important aspects like weed control, poultry and rainfed agriculture did not find place in the broadcast. Little less than one-fourth time was devoted to other aspects like budget, policy planning, forestry, environment and ecology and market management, etc.

The table provides a holistic view of programmes broadcast during June 1998. The data show that agronomy share was a major one; little less than one-fourth of all the topics broadcast. It has first place in all the three programmes, it was followed by plant protection with 13 per cent share; collectively both these subjects enjoyed more than one-third share in the broadcast programme. Ten per cent time of the broadcast was devoted to vegetable cultivation, soil and fertilizer management and orchard component of agriculture got 9.4 per cent time each.

Mushroom cultivation was totally neglected and could not find place in the broadcast, though it is very important area and finds favour with the farmers in the urban areas of Delhi, Gurgaon, Faridabad and Ghaziabad.

TABLE 3

Programme Categories and Time Devoted to Agricultural Programmes

S. No.	Programme category	Programme			Total	Rank
		Krishi Charcha	Unnat Krishi	Krishi Jagat		
1.	Agronomy	35	60	70	165 (23.9)	I
2.	Soil and fert-ilizer manage-ment	25	10	30	65 (9.4)	IV
3.	Plant protection	30	30	30	90 (13.0)	II
4.	Mushroom cultivation	-	-	-	-	
5.	Vegetables	20	30	20	70 (10.1)	III
6.	Orchards	15	40	10	65 (9.4)	V
7.	Weed mana-gement	5	10	-	15 (2.1)	XIII
8.	Animal husbandry	10	10	20	40 (5.7)	V
9.	Floriculture	-	-	10	10 (1.4)	X
10.	Poultry	5	10	-	15 (2.1)	VIII
11.	Fisheries	5	10	10	25 (3.6)	VI
12.	Rainfed agriculture	-	20	-	20 (2.9)	VII
13.	Piggery and goatry	-	10	10	20 (2.9)	VIII
14.	Agricultural engineering	-	10	-	10 (1.4)	IX
15.	Miscellaneous	-	10	70	80 (11.5)	

Figures in parentheses indicate percentage share of the total.

The farmers were of the view that the discussion mode of presentation, which also involves the farmer, is the best, followed by interview mode of presentation. Farmers also felt that topics like market news, weather forecast, *lok geet* in *Krishi Jagat* make it more interesting and attractive.

Regarding appropriateness of the broadcast timing during the day farmers were of the view that the *Krishi Jagat* Programme is best suited to the audience as it is broadcast in the evening, when farmers are free from field operations and are generally available at their homes. The morning programme *Krishi Charcha*, and the afternoon programme, *Unnat Krishi*, are quite often missed, as during these timings farmers are pre-occupied with their field and home activities.

In the changing agricultural scenario when need for information is increasing day by day and farmers are information hungry, radio can play a crucial role in providing them the desired information effectively and easily. To meet the farmers' requirement, programmes on agro-enterprises like poultry, piggery, mushroom cultivation, post-harvest magagement, value addition, bee keeping, protected vegetable cultivation, floriculture, etc. need to be given more and more emphasis in terms of quality and coverage.

To make the programmes more interesting and listener-friendly, appropriate mode of presentation, discussion or dramatic presentation may be adopted for effective transfer of technology for less articulate farmers.

2. A Critical Study of Farm Broadcasting at All India Radio, Chennai, Tamil Nadu

I. Dorairajan (1998)

Radio is one of the most important means of reaching the farmers. It is one of the fastest media and is becoming a powerful force for mobilising public opinion and for educating people in all spheres of life. The ultimate object of agricultural communication is that technology and agricultural news should reach the farmers. The message shold be clear to the farmers; it should be properly processed so that it is comprehensible, acceptable and motivate the farmers for adoption.

There are certain special advantages that radio has as a medium of communication. It reaches more people, moves more quickly than any other means of mass communication. It is relatively cheap and also reaches illiterate audiences. It builds enthusiasm and maintains interest. The medium has its limitations also—broadcasting facilities are available only in limited places, time assigned for radio talks is generally limited and it is difficult to check on results. The influence of radio is limited only to those who can listen intelligently. The programmes for rural people frequently lose out in competition with entertainment.

All the rural listeners may or may not be educated in the formal sense. Farmers do strenuous work throughout the day and like everyone else, would rather be entertained than educated after a day's hard work. Most of them do not take notes while listening to a programme. They value the radio as a source of news and other information, as a source of entertainment and company. They may not like to follow lengthy programmes unless the programmes hold exceptional interest. The rural listeners do not constitute a uniform type of audience. There are differences in education, age, income, experience, etc. The receptivity of the listeners to the programme depends upon their background and thus varies with the individuals. They have more interest in items of direct, timely and local interest to them. Many of them are faced with several problems and always in a mood to look forward to solutions for problems such as lack of food, clothing, housing, employment, health, etc. They try to stick up to their traditions, customs and culture.

The objectives of the study were : to critically study strategies adopted on the programming aspects of farm broadcast to identify constraints, if any, to suggest suitable measures for effective dissemination and to identify the needs of rural farmers.

The study was taken up to cover the farm broadcast

from AIR Chennai. Pre-tested questionnaires were used to collect data from AIR, extension workers and the farmers. The respondents were from four major districts of Tamil Nadu apart from minor representations from other districts. The farmers, extension officers and AIR officials were personally contacted and interviewed with the help of questionnaire prepared for this purpose.

The results of the present study showed that despite the availability of highly sophisticated and fast media like Video technology, Computer, Micro Computer technology and Internet, radio still reigns over the rural masses as a source of mass communication, be it for agro-technology or entertainment, regular news, etc. This fact is revealed in the present study as 87.6 per cent of the respondents possessed radio. Further the interest evinced in radio message by the rural people is reflected by the awareness of time of broadcast (94%) among the respondents.

Another interesting feature among the rural farmers is that they like to participate in programmes on radio and more so on television, for the personal appeal. In the present investigation nearly 60 per cent of the respondents had participated in the farm home programme.

As for the listening aspect, more than 55 per cent of the respondents listen daily. The impact of radio messages can be evaluated the way the medium has motivated the farmers in adoption of the messages. By way of motivation, it is interesting to note from the study that nearly 92 per cent of the respondents discussed the messages with their colleagues. To add up to this, it is surprising to learn that 93.8 per cent of the farmers have adopted what they hear from the radio.

Further it was observed that the illiterate radio listener is either equal to or higher than the literate one in communities without radios in terms of the level of general awareness. This observation clearly demonstrates the impact of radio even among the illiterate rural communities.

The present study also revealed the need for a sort of orientation training for the participants in radio talks. One skilled radio professional with a good tape recorder can produce high quality material for radio.

The economic well-being of the nation largely depends on agriculture and radio has attained the status of indispensable extension medium.

Generally, it is understood that the farmers are aware and interested in participating in the radio programme. Many of the farmers discuss the technology with their fellow farmers and it is encouraging to note that majority of the farmers are adopting the message they listen. From this study it is clear that farmers are interested in discussion and interviews rather than just talking along.

The study concludes that radio has been doing marvellous job in uplifting the rural masses. By following the suggested correctional measures, the efficiency can be further improved in the interest of national development.

3. A Study on the Sources of Information Used by Farmers in Mahendergarh District

Dr. R. S. Kanwar

Agricultural technology is transmitted to farmers through various media, personal localite or informal media, and personal cosmopolite or formal media. This project was planned to ascertain the sources of agricultural information used by the farmers in Mahendergarh district of Haryana with the following objectives : To explore the sources of agricultural information used by farmers, to compare the role of mass media with other sources used in dissemination of agricultural information, and to suggest suitable information strategy for the farmers of Mahendergarh district.

Mahendergarh is one of the oldest districts of Haryana; its landscape varies from flat to undulating, marked by sand dunes and small dry Aravali hills of varying heights. Fields suffer from water and wind erosion. Soils of the district are sandy to sandy loam with low organic matter. Water table is generally very deep with only 36 per cent of cultivable area under assured irrigation. It is considered to be an agriculturally backward district of Haryana. Small land holdings, poor irrigation facilities, poor economic conditions and lower literacy rate (44% as compared to 56% of Haryana) are some of the factors responsible for agricultural backwardness. These factors also directly affect the adoption of new farm technology by farmers. In general, lack of awareness, technical know-how and knowledge regarding resource factors such as credit, storage and marketing, etc. are the major reasons for non-adoption of technology by the farmers. A well developed communication system can help to improve the existing condition of lack of information.

A questionnaire was developed for the study and the data were collected by personally interviewing the farmers, both on soico-economic characters and use of media sources. The sources of information were categorised as under :

1. Mass media included television, radio, newspaper, agriculture literature, trainings, exhibitions, Kisan Melas (farmers' fairs) and demonstrations.
2. Interpersonal, external or formal sources included university and KGK, scientists, personnels of agriculture department, cooperative society, HSDC, NSC, HAFED, NEL, IFFCO, KRIBHCO, etc.
3. Interpersonal, local or information sources included neighbours, friends, progressive farmers, private dealers, relatives and family members.

The study revealed that whereas 42 per cent respondents had television sets and 24 per cent watched agriculture programme (*Krishi Darshan*), an earlier survey in five villages of this district showed use of TV by 11 per cent farmers. Radio was a more frequently used medium (58%). Majority of the respondents listen to evening programme (*Krishi Jagat*) from Rohtak station. Lack of time, interest and need-based programmes are some of the important reasons for not using television and radio, as mentioned by the farmers. Most of the farmers cannot adopt the information gained from these media sources because (i) they do not write down the information and hence forget them, and (ii) the questions arising in their minds remain unanswered for which they have to use interpersonal sources.

The other important sources of information used by the farmers to a great extent are demonstrations/ trainings/Kisan Melas and exhibitions. Field demonstrations, agricultural trainings, Kisan Melas, tours and exhibitions were used by 24, 20, 14 and 4 per cent respondents, respectively. Among interpersonal local sources, private dealers were used by maximum (92%) farmers followed by neighbours (80%), friends (56%) and progressive farmers (52%). Neighbours, friends and progressive farmers collectively serve as the most important localite source of agricultural information as 96 per cent respondents use these sources. To some extent, relatives (12%) and family members (8%) are also used as information sources.

TABLE 4

Sources of Agricultural Information Used by Farmers in Order of Preference

Source	Order of preference/utilization					
	First		Second		Third	
	Number	%	Number	%	Number	%
1. N/F/PF	27	54	13	26	12	24
2. Private dealer	8	16	21	42	15	30
3. Family member	2	4	2	4	0	0
4. Univ./Krishi Gyan Kendra	5	10	8	16	5	10
5. Agriculture Department	1	2	2	4	3	6
6. Haryana Seed Development Corporation/ Cooperative Societies	0	0	1	2	5	10
7. Radio	4	8	3	6	10	20
8. Agriculture literature	3	6	0	0	0	0
Total	50	100	50	100	50	100

N—Neighbours, F—Friends, PF—Progressive farmers.

Education has a marked effect on the use of media. About 93 per cent illiterate farmers used local sources for agricultural information, whereas educated farmers used all the three types of communication sources i.e. formal, informal and mass media sources. With the increase in education level dependence on local sources decreased. All the three categories of farmers (small, medium and big) used all types of sources viz., formal, informal and mass media; but big farmers used local sources less and mass media more than small or medium farmers.

On the basis of the study it was suggested that since farmers depend more on local sources, particularly neighbours, friends, progressive farmers and private dealers so the group leaders among these localites should be identified and made information rich so that agricultural technology can be effectively transmitted to 'information deficient' clientele. This can be done by training these progressive farmers and group leaders, and providing them literature on agriculture.

Local relay stations of T.V. and radio, and local newspapers can be very useful for meeting the requirements of farmers by providing them local and need-based programmes/material.

Agricultural literature should be made available in villages at some common places like Panchayat Bhawan, Farmers' Clubs, etc. so that interested readers can make use of it.

Demonstrations, trainings, exhibitions, etc. are quite effective and reliable sources of information. So, these methods should be used to the maximum extent.

4. Study of Influence of Doordarshan and Cable Network on Socio-Economic Parameters of Rural Households of Karnataka

P. V. Rama Gowda (1998)

The present study is an attempt to ascertain the socio-economic impact of TV viewing rural households in the Kolar district of Karnataka. The objectives of the study were : To analyse the association between the socio-economic parameters of TV owners of rural households. and to assess the influence of TV viewing on agriculture as well as on health and nutrition.

Sixty respondents were randomly selected from the TV owners of the two villages in Kolar district. A well structured pre-tested questionnaire was used to collect information from the sample respondents, and data obtained by contacting each of these respondents by personal interviews. The entire analysis was worked out separately for those two groups of respondents; first group comprising those who watch only Doordarshan and second group comprising those who watch both Doordarshan and cable network programmes. Simple tabular analysis with percentages was used to analyse the data.

The study revealed that TV viewing timings in rural areas ranged from 2-4 hours in case of those who watch Doordarshan programmes and ranged from 3-6 hours per day in case of those who watch both TV and cable programmes with an average time of 4.34 hours/day.

Regarding the viewing behaviour of the respondents, 68 per cent of the total respondents have indicated that they watch TV/cable for entertainment programme. This percentage is high in case of those who watch only Doordarshan programmes at 75 per ent (compared to 61% in cable network). About 55 per cent of all the respondents have indicated that they watch TV/cable in order to pass time and this percentage is high in case of those who watch cable network (64% against 47% in case of Doordarshan viewers).

The entire sample of households who had TV are literate indicating that most of literate households like to have TV in their homes. About 40 per cent of the total respondents in the rural households have collegiate education and more. The distribution of level of education in both groups of respondents was almost similar excepting higher education in case of those respondents who watch both TV and cable wherein all the respondents are from this category.

About 53 per cent of rural respondents have opined

that watching TV/cable has influenced the 'good living practice' and nearly equal number of respondents (52%) have also felt that the mass media has influenced positively regarding their knowledge of 'health awareness'. A moderate per cent of respondents (ranging from 35-41 per cent) in their opinion on the other health parameters under study such as 'tackling health problem', 'child nutrition' and 'child upkeep', have indicated that watching TV/cable has positive effect on their attitude towards health and nutrition.

Majority of rural respondents have opined after watching TV/cable network that there is an influence on the use of technologies in agriculture (65% of the respondents) and crops they are planning/growing (60%) and managing the diseases and pests (40%). Again about 43 per cent of the farmers indicated that watching TV provided information on markets as well as on price. On price forecasting, only about 12 per cent respondents positively opined that they were getting information on future prices of the commodities.

Annexure

THE RIGHT TO INFORMATION BILL 1997

A Bill to make provision for securing right to information which is a fundamental right being part of Article 19(1)(a) of the Constitution and for matters connected therewith or incidental thereto.

Be it enacted by Parliament in the forty eighth year of the Republic of India as follows

1. (1) The Act may be called the Right to Information Act, 1997.

(2) It extends to the whole of India.

It shall come into force on such date as Central Government may, by notification in the Official Gazette, appoint which shall not be later than 6 months from the date of the passing of the Act.

2. Definitions

In this Act, unless the context otherwise requires,

(a) "Information" means any material or information relating to the affairs, administration or conduct of public authority and includes any document or record relating to the affairs of the public authority'

(b) "prescribed" means prescribed by rules under the Act'

(c) "public authority" includes,

(i) the Government and Parliament of India and the Government and legislature of each of the States and of local or other authorities within the territory of India or under the control of the government of India; and

(ii) The administrative offices of the Courts.

(iii) a company, corporation, trust, firm, society, a cooperative society, or associations whether owned or controlled by the government or by private individuals and institutions;

The expressions company, corporation, trust, firm, society, cooperative society and association shall have the same meaning as assigned to them in the respective Acts under which they are registered.

(d) "right to information" means the right of access to information and includes the inspection, taking notes and extracts and obtaining certified copies of documents or records of any public authority'

(e) "State Government" includes the administrator of a Union Territory appointed by the President under Article 239 of the Constitution.

3. Right to Information

(1) Every citizen shall have a right to information from a public authority;

(2) Every public authority shall be under a duty to maintain all its records duly catalogued and indexed and subject to the provisions of section 4, to make available to any person requesting information from it, the information sought for, including such information as it is under an obligation to obtain and furnish and shall not withhold any information or limit its availability.

4. Obligations on Public Authorities

(1) Each public authority shall publish periodically, and keep updated, information indicating:

(i) particulars of its organization, functions and responsibilities;

(ii) description of its decision making processes in terms of procedures and powers and responsibilities of its officers and employees;

(iii) norms for performance of activities such as prescribed periods for their processing and completion of physical and financial targets, etc., and the actual achievements with reference to such norms;

(iv) classes of records under its control including the rules, regulations, instructions and list of manuals, etc. used by its employees for carrying out activities;

(v) the facilities provided for access to information; and

(vi) the name, designation and other relevant particulars of the Public Information Officer, to whom requests for information may be addressed.

(2) It shall also be the duty of the concerned officer's of a public authority to give reasons for decisions—whether administrative or adjudicative—to those affected and to disclose the relevant facts and analyses when major policies or decisions are announced.

(3) Nothing in the foregoing provisions of this section shall preclude the right of any person to obtain such information as would affect life or liberty of any persons in whom he is interested.

(4) It shall be mandatory for each custodial establishment such as a police lock-up, jail, mental asylum, remand house, women's home, beggars home, etcetera to appoint a visitors' committee comprising independent citizens which shall have full access to them at all hours of the day and night are to their records and inmates.

5. Restrictions on Right to Information

The public authority may, for reasons to be recorded in writing, withhold:

(a) information, the disclosure or contents of which will prejudicially affect the sovereignty and integrity of India, security of the State and friendly relations with foreign States, public order, investigation of an offence or which leads to incitement to an offence;

(b) information relating to personal or other information, the disclosure of which has no relationship to any public activity or in which the public has no interest and would constitute a clear and unwarranted invasion of personal privacy;

(c) trade and commercial secrets protected by law, provided that an appeal against the refusal of the information under clause (a) above, will lie to a Board headed by the Cabinet Secretary of the Government of India or the Chief Secretary of state government as the case may be and the Board shall dispose of the appeal within a period of 30 days from the receipt thereof.

Provided that information which cannot be denied to Parliament or State Legislature shall not be denied to any citizen.

6. Procedure for the Supply of Information

(1) A person desiring information from a public authority under this Act shall make an application to the person who shall be designated by the public authority for the purpose. For the said purpose the Official may be allowed to inspect the concerned document(s).

(2) The information asked for under sub-section (1) shall be furnished to the applicant by the public authority within thirty days of the application under sub-section (1), and where such information relates to the life or liberty of the individual, the information shall be supplied within forty-eight hours of the making of the application.

(3) The information asked for under sub-section (1) shall be supplied in writing either in English or Hindi or in the language of the State in which the public authority is located.

Provided that where a requester cannot for valid reasons, make a request in writing, the Public Information Officer may either accept an oral request or render reasonable assistance to the requester in making a written request.

(4) Every public authority shall have a right to charge fees for the supply of any document subject to the condition that such fees shall not exceed the cost of making and supplying the document.

7. Refusal to be Given in Writing

If the information asked for under sub-section (1) of Section 4 is refused by any public authority, the reasons for such refusal shall be given by such authority in writing.

8. Severability

If a request for access to information is refused on the ground that it is in relation to information which is withheld from disclosure, then notwithstanding any thing contained in this Act, access may be given to that part of the document which does not contain any information that is withheld from disclosure under this Act and which can reasonably be served from any part that contains withheld information. When only a part of the document is furnished, the reasons for withholding the rest of the document shall be given. If the information is refused, it shall be done so only with the approval of the higher Officer to be designated by the Public authority.

9. Appeal

An appeal against a refusal to furnish any document by a public authority under this Act shall lie to the District Judge or the Principal Civil Judge of the City Civil Court as the case may be of ordinary civil jurisdiction of the area in which the office of the public authority is located and any appeal shall be preferred within fifteen days of the date of refusal of the supply of information by the public authority and any appeal so preferred shall be disposed of by the Judge within thirty days of its filling, by a written order and giving reasons for its decision which shall be final.

10. Penalties

(1) Any individual responsible for providing any information under this Act shall be personally liable for furnishing the information within the period specified therein.

(2) Where the information asked for under this Act is

not furnished within the time specified, the person responsible for supplying the information shall be punishable or liable to pay personally a fine of rupees fifty for every day of delay after the day by which it is required to be supplied.

(3) If any person responsible for providing any information under this Act, fails to furnish such information or funishes any information which is false in any material particular and which he knows or has reasonable cause to believe to be false or does not believe it to be true, he shall be punishable or liable to pay personally a fine which shall not be less than rupees one thousand and which may extend to rupees five thousand.

Provided that the Court may, for reasons to be recorded in writing, levy a fine of less than one thousand rupees.

11. Offences by Companies & Societies, etc.

(1) Where an offence under this Act has been committed by a company, every person who, at the time the offence was committed, was in charge of, and was responsible to the company for the conduct of the business of the company, shall be deemed to be guilty of the offence and shall be liable to be proceeded against and punished accordingly:

Provided that nothing contained in this section shall render any such person liable to any punishment provided in this Act if he proves that the offence was committed without his knowledge or that he had exercised all due diligence to prevent the commission of such offence;

(2) Notwithstanding anything contained in sub-section (1) where an offence under this Act has been committed by a company and it is proved that the offence has been committed with the consent or connivance of or is attributable to any neglect on the part of any director, manager, secretary or other officer of the company, such director, manager,

secretary, or officer shall also be deemed to be guilty of that offence and shall be liable to be proceeded against and punished accordingly.

Explanation : For the purposes of this section,

(a) "company" means any body corporate, and includes a firm or association of individuals; and

(b) "director" in relation to a firm means a partner of the firm.

12. Offences to be Cognizable

Notwithstanding anything contained in the code of Criminal Procedure 1973, every offence under this Act shall be cognizable.

13. Notwithstanding anything contained in this Act or in any other law for the time being in force, it shall be the duty of every public authority which proposes to initiate any project or activity, subject to the provisions of section 4, to notify, as soon as possible, and in any case well before the commencement of the project or activity, for the information of the general public and the persons to be affected, such matters within its knowledge and control as affect the general public or are vital to life, health and livelihood.

14. Protection of Action Taken in Good Faith

No suit, prosecution or other legal proceeding shall lie against the Central Government or a State Government or any individual, for anything which is in good faith done or intended to be done under the provisions of this Act or any rule made thereunder.

15. Act to have Overriding Effect

The provisions of this Act shall have affect notwithstanding anything inconsistent therewith contained in any other law for the time being in force.

16. National Council for Freedom of Information

(1) The Central Government may, by notification in the Official Gazette, establish with effect from such

day as may be specified in the notification, a Council to be known as the National Council for Freedom of Information.

(2) The National Council may consist of the following members :

(a) the Minister in charge of Department of Administrative Reforms in the Central Government, who shall be its Chairman, and

(b) such other official and non-official members drawn from different disciplines such as Law, Education Media, Science & Technology, Social Activists, Business.

3. (a) the Council may meet as and when necessary, with atleast one meeting being held every four months;

(b) the time and place of the meetings of the Council shall be as the Chairman thinks fit and it shall observe such procedure as may be prescribed to transact its business.

17. Objects of the National Council

The object of the National Council shall be to promote freedom of information in the country and it shall deal with all matters related to freedom of information such as

(a) review of the operation of the Act and rules made thereunder,

(b) review of the administrative arrangements and procedures to secure for citizens the fullest possible access to information,

(c) research and documentation as regards management of information with a view to improving the extent and accuracy of information being made available under the Act, and

(d) to advise the government on all matters related to freedom of information, including training, development and orientation of employees to bring in a culture of openness and transparency.

(e) there shall be a statutory Parliamentary Committee on the Right to Information to review the implementation of the Act.

18. State Councils for Freedom of Information

(1) The State Government may, by notification in the Official Gazette, establish with effect from such day as may be specified in the notification, a Council to be known as the State Council for Freedom of Information.

(2) The State Council may consist of the following members :

(a) the Minister in charge of Department of Administrative Reforms in the State Government, who shall be its Chairman, and

(b) such other official and non-official members drawn from different disciplines such as Law, Education, Science & Technology, Media, Social Activities and Business.

3(a) the Council may meet as and when necessary, with at least one meeting being held every four months.

(b) the time and place of the meeting of the Council shall be as the Chairman thinks fit and it shall observe such procedure as may be prescribed to transact its business.

19. Objects of the State Council

The object of the State Council shall be to promote the freedom of information within the State and it shall deal with the matters specified in section 18 in respect of the State. The State Council shall present its report annually to the State Legislature.

20. Power of the Central Government to Make Rules

(1) The Central Government may, by notification in the Official Gazette, make rules to carry out the provision of this Act.

(2) Without prejudice to the generality of the foregoing power, such rules may provide for all matters in respect of which rules are required to be made by the Central Government under this Act.

21. Power of the State Government to Make Rules

A State Government may, by notification in the Official Gazette, make rules to provide for any matter in respect of which rules are required to be made by the State Government under this Act.

22. Laying of Rules

(1) Every rule made under this Act by the Central Government shall be laid, as soon as may be after it is made, before each House of Parliament, while it is in session, for a total period of thirty days which may be comprised in one session or in two or more successive sessions and if, before the expiry of the session immediately following the session or the successive sessions aforesaid, both Houses agree in making any modification in the rule, or both Houses agree that the rule should not be made, the rule shall thereafter have effect only in such modified form or be of no effect, as the case may be; so, however, that any such modification or annulment shall be without prejudice to the validity of anything previously done under that rule.

(2) Every rule made under this Act by a State Government shall be laid, as soon as may be after it is made, before the State Legislature.

REFERENCES

Doordarshan (1993). Television and its Impact on Rural Areas—A Doordarshan Study. In : (eds.) Dua, M. R. and Gupta, V. S., *Media and Development*. Har-Anand Publications, New Delhi.

Grassroots (1999). Reporting the human condition (1-7). Press Institute of India, New Delhi.

Gupta, V. S. (1996). Media Strategies for Rural Development. In: *Kurukshetra*, Vol. XLIV, No. 4-5.

Gupta, V. S. (1989). Case Study of Indian Rural Television. The Krishi Darshan Programme. *Media Asia* 16 (4) : 215-218.

Gupta, V.S. and Rajeshwar Dayal (eds.) (1995). *Rural Press—Problems and Prospects*. Concept Publishing Company, New Delhi.

P. Sainath (1996). *Everybody Loves a Good Drought, Stories from India's Poorest Districts*. Penguin Books, India, New Delhi.

P. Sainath (1998). Fact and Fiction in *Exploring the Heartland, An Agenda for the media*. Press Institute of India. New Delhi.

Voices (1997). Consultation on Media Policy and Community Radio. Workshop Report, Bangalore.

6

Health, Population and Communication Strategy

The following excerpt from the memorable speech of Jawahar Lal Nehru in the Constituent Assembly on 14 August 1947 gives us a glimpse of what the founding fathers of the Indian independence movement had envisioned for the country

> *Long ago we made a tryst with destiny, and now the time comes when we shall redeem our pledge... The achievement we celebrate today is but a step, an opening of opportunity, to the great triumphs and achievements that await us..... the ending of poverty and ignorance and disease and inequality of opportunity.*

Article 47 of the Indian Constitution says : The state shall regard the raising of the level of nutrition and the improvement of public health as among its primary duties.

The above stipulation, a part of Directive Principles of the Indian Constitution envisages fixing certain social and economic goals for immediate attainment to fulfil the basic needs of the common man. Let us see to what extent the above goals have been achieved in respect of health and population sector.

India has :

(i) the highest number of T.B. patients in the world, and growing
(ii) the highest number of malaria deaths
(iii) the highest number of blind people
(iv) the highest number of HIV positive cases
(v) the highest number of occupational casualties
(vi) the highest number of hepatitis B patients
(vii) one of the highest infant and maternal mortality rates
(viii) one of the highest incidences of malnutrition.
(ix) sixty per cent of all births are attended by untrained persons in rural India.

Despite concerted efforts India continues to record high levels of morbidity, especially among infants, children, the elderly and women. The burden of short duration and major morbidity falls on the vulnerable sections of the population, including wage labourers, minorities and the low income groups *(India : Human Development Report NCAER, 1999)*.

In his Convocation Address at the All India Institute of Medical Sciences in July 1998, the Prime Minister, Mr. Atal Behari Vajpayee said that our record in health care was far from edifying and called for a radical reform in both health care and medical education systems to ensure that the advances in medicine that had taken place and the vast infrastructure for health care created over the past five decades were made accessible to the masses at affordable cost.

What has caused concern is that now there is increasing morbidity due to non-communicable diseases and newly emerging infections such as HIV. Expressing concern over the state of affairs, the Approach Paper to the Ninth Five Year Plan (1997-2002) says : Communicable diseases continue to be a major cause of morbidity and mortality in India. In addition to the existing bacterial, viral and parasitic infections, there are newer additions such as HIV infection, re-emergence of some infections such as *kala azar*, so that the disease burden due to communicable diseases continues to be very high. There are National Programmes for control of vector borne diseases, tuberculosis, leprosy and HIV infection. The performance in many of these has been suboptimal, an important factor being the lack of key personnel such as lab technicians and multipurpose workers. The morbidity due to communicable and nutrition-related diseases has not shown a parallel decline; in addition, there is now an increasing morbidity due to non-communicable diseases and newly emerging infections.

The situation is dismal because the Indian government, over the years has not spent more than 1.8 per cent of GDP on health. The current figure of public spending is 1.3 per cent of GDP. Nicaragua spends 6.7, Brazil 2.8 and China 2.1 per cent. Among the advanced industrial nations, Sweden spends 7.9 and the United States 5.6 per cent. When newly independent, India committed 5 per cent of the outlay of her first five year plan to health. In a nation emerging from over a century of colonial rule, exploitation, famines and mass deaths from disease, this was and is vital step, but this has come down to 1.7 per cent by the eighth five year plan, falling with each successive plan. In terms of health infrastructures, countries like China and Sri Lanka are way ahead of India[1].

It is indeed a sad commentary on the topsy turvy priorities in the working of our planning process that India produces more doctors than nurses and exports thousand of doctors. Surprisingly in 1990, there were 381,978 registered allopathic doctors, but only 111,235 nurses in the country. According to Prime Minister P. V. Narasimha Rao, the country produces 14,000 doctors, but only 8,000 nurses a year (September 1995).

One of the major challenges in the 21st century is to enhance the outlay for health, ensure its equitable distribution between states, narrow the rural urban gap and remove the lacunae impeding effective delivery of health care services at the community level, both in rural and urban areas. A sizeable population living in slums has no access to affordable medicare despite proliferation

---

1. P. Sainath, 1996.

of private practitioners, nursing homes and corporate hospitals.

This record of national health achievement has, however, certain extenuating features. The brightest of the achievements is dramatic improvement in life expectancy, before independence the average life expectancy was less than thirty years; today a baby born in India can hope to live twice as long. Likewise the rate of infant mortality has been reduced to less than half of what it was in 1945, just before independence. Smallpox has been eradicated and cholera epidemics have been controlled.

The overall picture, by and large, remains highly unsatisfactory.

Health is an indicator of well-being that has direct implications not only for the quality of life but also indirect implications for the production of economic goods and services. 'Health for All by the Year 2000' was a national goal set by Indian policy-makers over 20 years ago in Alma Ata.[2] Since then a lot of planning, effort and public expenditure have gone into improving human health both in rural and urban India. The spread of accessibility to modern medicine has improved substantially across the country. Despite concerted efforts, however, India continues to be among the many developing countries of the world with high levels of morbidity, especially among infants, children, women, and the elderly.

There is also a high incidence of communicable diseases normally associated with low levels of sanitation and public hygiene, poor quality of drinking water and under-nutrition.

In this context the Nobel laureate Indian economist Amartya Sen has noted the thorough going *underactivity of the government* in the health sector and has supported

2. A global initiative towards health-related research and action was taken at an international conference on Primary Health Care held in Alma Ata (in the erstwhile USSR) in 1978. In its Declaration, the conference spelt out the goal of the signatory nations which was to ensure 'Health for All by the Year 2000' with primary health care as its top priority.

effective government intervention in this sector. Sen says There are many failures, particularly in the development of public educational facilities, health care provisions, social security arrangements, local democracy, environmental protection, and so on, and the stifling of market incentives is only one part of that larger picture. The failures can, thus, be scarcely seen simply as the result of an 'overactive' government. That can be justifiably seen as overactivity in some fields has been inseparably accompanied by thorough going *underactivity* in others. ......Among the different forms of interventions that can contribute to the provision of social security, the role of health care deserves forceful emphasis. Illness is, obviously enough, one of the most widespread causes of human deprivation and economic insecurity in India. It affects not only the actual patients and those who depend on them for their subsistence, but also other members of the society, in so far as the *threat* of disease arising from widespread morbidity reduces the quality of life. Further, the limitations of private provision in the domain of health care are well known. A well-developed system of public health is an essential contribution to the fulfilment of social security objectives[3].

This is one field where there is an overwhelming need for bold initiatives and comprehensive reform. Compared with many other developing countries, India has poor health achievements despite spending a comparatively large part of its GNP on health (if one adds up public and private spending). Much of this mismatch between resources and achievements is due to the poor functioning of the public health care system, especially in rural areas. In some states, this system is little more than a collection of deserted primary health centres, filthy dispensaries, unmotivated doctors, and chaotic hospitals. Paradoxically despite the improvement in health infrastructure, many citizens, mostly in rural areas are deprived of basic health care. A chunk of health budget goes to urban hospitals at the expense of primary health care or services in rural

---

3. *India : Economic Development and Social Opportunity (1996).*

areas. The situation in rural areas is so dismal that there is one doctor for 20 odd villages, or over 20,000 people in parts of the country.

Through these various interconnections, education and health can be variables of great strategic importance in the process of economic development. India's failure to have an adequate public policy in educational and health matters can be, thus, of profound significance in assessing the limited success of Indian development efforts over the last half a century.

Reproductive Health

Ever since the inception of family planning programme, one of the serious deficiencies has been that reproductive health component of health service was completely ignored. It was only as a result of Programme of Action of the International Conference on Population and Development (ICPD), 1994 that the Reproductive and Child Health (RCH) programme was launched in October 1997[4]. Under this programme a comprehensive package of services for family planning, maternal and child health plan has been envisaged. Large scale assistance from the World Bank and other donor agencies has been committed for its successful implementation.

A special edition of *Voices* (Vol. III, No. 2), 1995 was devoted to highlighting Programme of Action of ICPD, and explaining in detail various aspects of reproductive health, which constitutes an essential part of our understanding of health and population issues in the country.

The current focus on reproductive health marks a global recognition that reproductive health needs have been largely neglected. Consequently this neglect has had profound adverse impact particularly for women.

Reproductive health encompasses a range of health concerns, yet there remains some confusion about what really constitutes reproductive health, how it differs from ongoing MCH/FP programmes and why there is a need

---

4. India 1999.

for a broad reproductive health orientation to the family planning policies in India.

The International Conference on Population and Development, defined reproductive health as "a state of complete physical, mental and social well-being and not merely the absence of disease or infirmity, in all matters relating to the reproductive system and to its functions and processes." In short, a reproductive health orientation, drawn from this and other sources, includes :

1. a satisfying and safe sex life free from the fear of disease and free from coercion and violence,
2. the capability to reproduce, and the freedom to decide if, when and how often, to do so, that is, access to both infertility services on the one hand and contraceptive services on the other,
3. access to safe and affordable abortion facilities,
4. reproductive choice for women and men; that people have the right to be informed and have access to safe, effective, affordable and acceptable methods of family planning of their choice,
5. safe child-bearing: access to appropriate health care services that will enable women to go safely through pregnancy and child birth and provide for a healthy infant,
6. access to services for the prevention and care of reproductive health problems, both gynaecological and obstetric, in a culturally sensitive manner,
7. Special attention to adolescents whose reproductive health needs have been particularly overlooked. Whatever the criterion, the available evidence points to poor reproductive health among women in India.

Despite the interest in women's reproductive health in India, information on the reproductive health situation continues to be incomplete and patchy. Lot of data are available on one aspect of reproductive health i.e. contraceptive use patterns but there is almost no information available on the prevalence of reproductive tract infections, abortion related morbidity and infertility.

Safe motherhood is still a dream for much of India and particularly for its rural areas. Few women have access to ante-natal care, the recent NFHS study shows that only half of all rural women were immunised against tetanus only two in five have received an ante-natal check up from a doctor or other health professionals and only 45 per cent received iron supplementation. As a result, high risk cases go undetected, anaemia is widespread, and knowledge of health and nutrition needs during pregnancy and the post-natal period are poorly understood

Access to safe delivery is equally poor : three in four rural Indian women continue to be delivered by untrained attendants in unhygienic conditions (Kanitkar and others, 1994). It is no surprise, therefore, that maternal deaths account for a large proportion of all deaths of women of reproductive age; more among rural women. Maternal mortality levels in India remain among the highest in the world estimated at between 420-555 per 100,000 live births.

Much more pervasive is reproductive morbidity and lack of care during pregnancy and childbirth including both, and the obstetric as well as gynaecological conditions, such as reproductive tract infections, cervical cell changes and genital prolapse. Health facilities at the community level are poorly equipped to deal with gynaecological and obstetric morbidities since they have neither the diagnostic facilities nor the drugs to treat them. Moreover, service providers are not trained to detect such morbidities nor to provide sensitive counselling. What is needed at the primary health centre level are facilities for routine diagnosis, improved obstetric care, sensitive counselling and sound referral services.

Regarding access to safe and affordable abortion services, it is found that roughly five million abortions continue to be performed annually, of these about 0.6 million abortions are performed under health services network. The growing tendency to misuse sophisticated prenatal diagnostic technique to abort female foetuses, suggests the disturbing possibility of increased abortions and repeat abortions. Safe abortion services are available only in urban areas. There is no information and counselling about legal termination services available to rural women, there is limited publicity about the law and there is widely held perception that abortion is illegal.

Little is known about the levels and patterns or consequences of infertility in India. Factors underlying infertility include women's poor health and nutrition status which can lead to repeated miscarriages and foetal wastages, unhygienic obstetric and abortion procedures, STDs and even tuberculosis. The health services are scarcely comprehensive enough to provide access to reliable information, sympathetic counselling and services to infertile couples. What is required is a sound referral system for infertile couples, alongwith primary health care which can provide basic information and counselling.

Although more than two in five couples in the reproductive age use a method of contraception, there is little informed choice in the matter of contraception. Programme priorities promote female sterilisation and as a result of the emphasis on terminal contraception, young and low parity women remain unprotected from repeated and closely-spaced pregnancies which enhance chances of reproductive morbidity.

The focus on sterilisation, target fulfilment and incentives has resulted in obscuring the spacing needs of women and their right to exercise an informed choice. Service delivery strategies and quality of care have been largely insensitive to the needs of women, the constraints the average woman faces in seeking services, in voicing fears and side-effects and their right to have complete pre-acceptance counselling, including information on potential side effects and complications and post acceptance followup.

Adolescent girls are particularly vulnerable and neglected, coming under the purview of government programmes only when they are pregnant. The majority are out of school and are neither serviced by educational or school health programmes nor by child health and nutrition services. At the family level too, girls are highly vulnerable : Son preference is pervasive, resulting in gender disparities in health care, food intake, school attendance and child labour from an early age. Complications of pregnancy, pre-natal and neo-natal mortality and low birth weight are much higher among adolescent women than among older women.

Increasing sexual activity cambined with ignorance about safe sex is a particularly alarming combination in the light of the HIV epidemic. It is time that sex education programmes became more realistic in terms of information needs of adolescents and youth both in and out of school.

The health delivery system has been largely insensitive to the reproductive health care needs of women and constraints they face in expressing these— let alone the constraints they face in obtaining services. Doorstep services are essential for secluded women and these are rarely undertaken, and where undertaken, focus more on contraception than on reproductive health in general. A comprehensive focus on adolescent girls mostly out of school to improve their nutritional levels, access to health services, information, vocational skills development and increase their ages at marriage would meet an important health needs at an early stage in the life cycle.

Health workers themselves are poorly informed about reproductive morbidity, can be insensitive in probing and are preoccupied with achieving contraceptive targets rather than offering a range of reproductive health services. *The poor reproductive health situation in India and particularly that of the Indian women calls for a broad reproductive health programme and a women-centred orientation.* Strategies and programmes to empower women in terms of control of economic resources, information and education, their rights, as well as in terms of self-confidence and ability to recognise, articulate and seek care for health problems are necessary conditions enabling the enhancement of women's health and rights. It has now been clearly established that CBR[5] in the southern states in India is relatively low ranging from 21 in Kerala

---

5. Crude Birth Rate (CBR) is defined as number of live births in a given period for a total population of one thousand.

to 28 per thousand in Tamil Nadu, compared to the highest in Rajasthan at 44 per thousand population. The low CBR among the southern states may be due to higher age at marriage, higher levels of female literacy and wider use of contraception among the population.

Population Policy

By common consent, the greatest failure since independence has been our inability to prevent the exponential increase in population. With the present alarming growth of population, it is unrealistic to expect the state of nation to improve, poverty to be alleviated and unemployment to be contained. As India enters the 21st century with one billion population, it is indeed a disturbing thought that we have over 300 million people who live below the poverty line and go hungry to bed every night. The state of deprivation for such a large chunk of population could not have gone further. India has more than 400 million uneducated people, with mounting problems of unemployment, lack of shelter, poverty, malnutrition; this situation in the ultimate analysis likely to result in a revolt against the present system. When the situation is assessed against the fact that government of India was the first in the world to initiate a comprehensive Family Planning programme in the world in 1951, the failure of the programme to control population does raise a question mark as to where and how we had gone wrong.

The health statistics are depressing enough; and if we also look at the problem of exploding population—a billion and beyond—we find ourselves situated in an inextricably difficult condition.

India's family planning programme provides a glaring example of dissonance between the use and development of the technology for reproductive control and other major variables which constitute the entire system. Decision makers held a strong conviction that an ideal contraceptive is the key to solving the population problem of the country. They ignored the fact that action for demand-generation and the development of an efficient and effective delivery system are the more crucial variables of the system. The privileged classes, who dominate the decision-making process, have been lukewarm towards the developmental programmes which are crucial to demand generation. This resulted in their totally unrealistic expectations about the development of technology for reproduction control.

It is now generally accepted that the target oriented, heavy handed approach, with an element of coercion created an adverse impact; and a mind set which was not conducive to successful implementation of the programme. The programme, instead of becoming a people's movement and people's concern, became a pre-occupation which concerned the government alone. In a study, *From Population to People* (1988), Ashish Bose says : bulldozing does not make a programme a people's programme. On the contrary, it comes in the way of people's participation....the people are alienated by the family planning programme; they are angry with insensitive officials who are administering this programme; they are critical of unhelpful politicians who make speeches in the name of the people; the doctors feel humiliated at the treatment given to them by the higher bureaucracy, both medical and non-medical; the multipurpose workers feel harassed at the sterilisation quota allotted to them. But the number game in New Delhi goes on.....targets are set and targets are achieved in rows of statistical figures presented in the government reports. How long will this number game go on? For whom will the target toll?

Since the issue of bringing down the birth rate of population continues to be a constant pre-occupation with the government administrators and planners, there has been recently discussion, as to why China's achievement in bringing down birth rate over a short period through coercive measures may not be adopted in India as well.

The policy planners in India would do well to heed to the note of caution administered by Amartya Sen who says : It is not clear how the acceptability of coercion can be tested except through democratic confrontation. While that testing has not occurred in China, it was indeed attempted in India during the Emergency[6] period in the seventies when compulsory birth control was tried by Mrs. Gandhi's government, alongwith suspending various legal rights and civil liberties. The policy of coercion in general—including that in birth control—was overwhelmingly defeated in the general elections that followed. Furthermore, family-planning experts have noted how voluntary birth-control programmes received a severe set-back from that brief programme of compulsory sterilization, as people had become deeply suspicious of the entire movement. The coercive measures of the Emergency period, in fact, aside from having little immediate impact on fertility rates, were followed by a long period of *stagnation* in the birth rate, which only ended in 1985.

There is evidence that some forms of compulsion or forceful pressure to accept birth control (especially sterilization) continue to be used in some Indian states, particularly in the north, where fertility rates tend to be high. Even when coercion is not a part of official policy, the government's firm insistence on 'meeting the family planning targets' often leads administrators and health-care personnel at different levels to resort to all kinds of pressure tactics that come close to compulsion. Some of the instances generally reported by the family welfare personnel are : verbal threats, making sterilization a condition of eligibility for anti-poverty programmes, depriving mothers with more than two children of maternity benefits, reserving certain kinds of health care services to persons who have more than two children from contesting panchayat elections. The long-run consequences of these practices can be quite disastrous both for health care and for the consensual emergence of social norms favouring smaller families.

There are, however, certain redeeming features to the intractable problem of increasing birth rate—female literacy, enhanced status of women, and the movement

6. The Janta government, which came to power after the Emergency, changed the nomenclature of the Ministry from Family Planning to Family Welfare.

for women empowerment would go a long way in easing India's population problem. The world over, rising female literacy has been accompanied by lower birth rates and enhanced social and economic indices. The link between female literacy and fertility is particularly evident. This linkage has been widely observed in other countries, and it is not surprising that it should emerge in India too. The unwillingness of educated women to be tied down to continuous child-rearing clearly plays a role in bringing about this attitudinal change. Education also makes the horizon of vision wider, and, at a more mundane level, helps to disseminate the knowledge of family planning. The Indian policy making will have to consider population problem not so much in terms of population control, but in terms of strong, positive, societal measures which essentially means better education, skill-development and, improved health care alongwith dignity and empowerment for women.

The role of voluntary organisations in a mass movement such as population control is critical for generation of momentum and accelerating the pace of progress. There is a need to incorporate family planning as a major objective of all voluntary organisations concerned with health and/or education-related activities. Substantially increased amount of funds need to be channelised through these agencies. The establishment of an apex organisation to develop networking between all such voluntary organisations committed to the promotion of national efforts in this important area of human endeavour need to be considered earnestly.

It is impossible to conceive the successful implementation of a vast national programme of family welfare without the cooperation of local bodies, particularly panchayati raj institutions, voluntary and non-governmental organisations. It is generally conceded that no government can build a society, whereas voluntary action can. The voluntary bodies have more freedom to articulate their point of view, raise consciousness, motivate and mobilise people. With greater involvement of the people in the population control and family planning programmes through the Panchayati Raj System as envisaged in the Constitution (Seventy-Second Amendment) Bill 1991, the programme will become one of "people's operation with government cooperation". The health planners and administrators must not only become sensitive and responsive to the felt needs of the people but must also adapt to the instrumentality of local self-government.

The functions of voluntary development organisations have changed over the years such as (a) relief and welfare, (b) community development, (c) sustainable system, and (d) people's movement. NGO-role changed as doer, mobiliser, catalyst and activist. Managerial approach to development also passed through logistic management and self-management over the years. Organisations are strategic if they contribute directly to long term objectives of the society. NGOs have strategic roles in catalysing transformation, checking abuses of power, facilitating reconciliation and providing essential community services. New roles demand new competencies from NGOs to act as advocates, educators, catalysts, monitors, mediators, etc[7].

In the health and population sector several voluntary and non-governmental organisations have made commendable contribution in reaching the unreached areas and sections of population where government efforts could not have accomplished the desired objectives.

The Voluntary Health Association of India (VHAI)—a non-profit federation of over 3000 organisations, has been working in the area of health and community development, strives to make health a reality for all. The VHAI fulfils these objectives primarily through training and by providing information to the target groups. It campaigns on relevant and important health issues to ensure that a people oriented health policy is brought about and effectively implemented.

The Family Planning Association of India (FPAI), an NGO with national status, links 2297 NGOs working in diverse fields to promote reproductive health including

---

7. *Kurukshetra*, October 1998.

family planning and gender equality. Its branch units are also actively involving local NGOs and community groups. The orientation programmes conducted by FPAI include individual and group counselling activities, in-house courses for volunteers and staff at various levels to enhance knowledge and competence levels. Family welfare programme, which needs resurrection, can succeed through an approach which is primarily non-governmental and people oriented. Since the Association has most of its projects in rural areas, it has been able to provide access to health services so as to motivate eligible couples to space out the number of children.

The Kerala Sastra Sahitya Prisad, whose contribution in developing literacy campaigns has already been outlined, is one of the few NGOs which has attempted to demystify medicine. Special campaigns on the drug policy, anti-smoking and amniocentesis have had some limited impact, both at the policy level as well as in educating the consumers. The KSSP emphasises that the greatest health problem is poverty and that the majority of ailments arise from the inadequacy of proper food and an unhealthy living environment. It has organised numerous health camps, published several documents on people's health, and are in constant touch with various organisations like the Voluntary Health Association of India. The KSSP believes that health care is a basic right of every citizen and an effective health care delivery system should work towards keeping the entire population physically and mentally healthy. It warns people against the modern health care systems controlled by multinational drug companies, stressing instead the wealth of knowledge that exists in traditional systems of medicine.

A major cause of our failure to achieve fuller and quicker results in our family planning and health programmes lies in the failure of communication. The fact that large sections of our rural population have upto now been almost inaccessible, except to their neighbourhood groups, because of remote location, illiteracy and lack of communication infrastructure, except for radio; has certainly made the success of the programme difficult. It has remained a government programme, the community's active involvement and participation being marginal. Due to inadequacy of Information, Education and Communication (IEC) activities the knowledge of the community about the contraceptives, their availability, safety, etc. are at a low level. Adoption of the small family norm and use of appropriate measures for birth control are matters of personal choice and decision.

Information, Education and Communication, which are critical inputs need to be further strengthened and expanded. Greater use of the mass media need be made to disseminate the message of family planning to the remotest corner of the country and the entire system of pricing the media time vis-a-vis its social responsibility has to be given a fresh look, different from the commercial angle. Area specific IEC material can be developed and produced only if efforts are made to pool resources of various social sectors and to provide community TV/radio sets, besides maintaining them. The backbone of the IEC efforts will, however, remain the inter-personal communication for which the grassroot level female worker will have to be trained and effectively utilised.

Family Planning must be projected not in narrow technical terms, but as *an enabling transforming force* which represents the ability of human being to take a conscious decision and control the course of life. The message of family planning cannot be given in isolation—it is an integral part of the effort to better the human condition and therefore must be integrated with other development messages. It is also essential to carry out intensive communication campaign for communities that are lagging behind in family planning acceptance. Such a campaign need to be culture and value specific.

Evolving an effective communication strategy for family welfare programmes is no simple, academic task; for here the communication experts have an extremely challenging responsibility to perform; which involves changing the mind set of the people or as the eminent communication scholar, Kiran Karnik says : Creating change, Change, especially of deeply ingrained values and beliefs, is extremely difficult, and for mass media to create such a change, is indeed a tall order. However, if the effort is dovetailed with other uses of media (especially agenda setting/ambience creation and education/training), it may be possible to initiate or trigger a process of change.

Let us have a look at the rural segment— with its rigid social structure, belief in early female marriage, preference for son (instances where mother is forced to have repeated pregnancies even after the birth of several daughters continue to proliferate except in literate families), gender discrimination, unwillingness to send girls for education or jobs (particularly in BIMARU[8] states)—all these pose serious impediments for a communication expert to cross over; for him it is not a question of media use—print or broadcast, channel—local, national or global; the question will always be to create a message which is attuned to his mind set, in consonance with his socio-economic profile and which does not make him merely a beneficiary of government programmes; but a stack holder in it.

Fortunately during the Sixth Plan period, communication strategies were redefined bringing in issues such as beyond 'family planning factors' which included programmes for child survival, improving the status of women, literacy and others. The major interventions initiated in the Eighth Five Year Plan were with the objectives of (a) inducing a shift in values, attitudes, and behaviour patterns regarding health and health-related issues. Specific programme indicators such as reduction in infant and maternal mortality, universal immunization, coverage of pregnant mothers and infants, increased number of deliveries by trained hands, better utilization of health services and, lastly, reduction in family size by a healthy mix of spacing and terminal methods; (b) mobilizing people, NGOs, and the government machinery through the process of community participation by instituting women's groups in the villages known as *Mahila*

8. Bihar, Madhya Pradesh, Rajasthan and Uttar Pradesh.

Mandals was also to be undertaken and (c) involvement of non-governmental organizations in health communication and training.

In a pioneering study of coverage of health and nutrition issues in print media and the readership behaviour of the respondents, Saroj Dahiya concludes that the coverage of health and nutrition issues suffers from inadequacy and distortion. Issues like food quality control, and nutrition during life cycle were totally ignored in all the selected dailies, whereas topics like recent health/nutrition care and techniques occupied maximum space followed by cookery/recipes, advances in food science and technology, epidemiology and management of diseases and nutritional quality of foods in all the newspapers. The important issues i.e. role of food in health/nutrition schemes introduced by government received meagre coverage in all the papers. Press correspondents of the papers and freelance journalists were important source of information about health and nutrition topics.

Role of food in health and disease, advances in food science and technology, recent health/nutrition care and techniques, foods in advertisements, cookery/recipes were some other topics preferred by majority of the respondents followed by issues i.e. health/nutrition programmes and epidemiology and management of diseases in different newspapers. Sixty per cent respondents made it clear that gender makes no difference in reporting health and nutrition issues. Table 5 analyses the space covered, and different categories of health and nutrition issues, in selected English dailies.

TABLE 5

Space Covered by Different Categories of Health and Nutrition Issues in Selected English Dailies

S. No.	Categories of health and nutrition	The Hindustan Times (col. cms)	The Times of India (col. cms)	The Indian Express (col. cms)	The Hindu (col. cms)	The Tribune (col. cms)	Total space
1.	Role of food in health and diseases	—	22.15	21.30	16.22	—	59.67
2.	Cookery/recipes	18.22	23.70	30.12	25.30	26.72	124.06
3.	Present food trends	17.22	—	—	—	—	17.22
4.	Recent health/nutrition care and techniques	22.07	33.75	24.25	32.76	30.20	143.03
5.	Health and nutrition programmes	25.15	15.65	16.52	24.19	—	81.51
6.	Advances in food science and technology	24.15	18.85	16.52	35.25	28.15	122.92
7.	Foods in advertisements	18.30	—	18.72	17.12	24.91	79.05
8.	Epidemiology and management of diseases	21.72	—	22.13	32.34	36.72	112.91
9.	Nutritional qualities of foods	33.90	—	20.13	—	26.10	80.13
10.	Food quality, control and malpractices	17.27	—	10.12	18.82	—	46.21
11.	Nutrition during life cycle	—	—	12.19	—	26.20	38.39
	Total space covered (col. cms)	198	114	192	202	199	905

Majority of the respondents suggested to cover sufficient aspects like food quality control, role of food in health and disease, advances in food science and technology, and nutritional quality of foods; more in number and space to enhance the knowledge regarding these issues. It was further suggested that all the news should be reported timely, objectively, in well summarised form based on actual research in depth in the form of articles, interviews with scientists, news, advertisements and features. Health and nutritional status of people in rural areas may also be adequately covered.

Saroj Dahiya suggests that : (i) The coverage of health and nutrition news should be increased. All newspapers should give one-third part (both in number and space) daily to such reporting. The newspapers should regularly take an active part in covering the process of development; (ii) While covering the news/features about various development programmes, reporter should try to make direct contact with those people who are supposed to be the real beneficiaries of such programmes. Such an attempt would provide true information about various development programmes; (iii) Health reporting of rural areas and of various health and nutrition programmes should be increased and (iv) Latest updated news on health and nutrition should be given in the newspapers. It should be based on research conducted. The newspapers should regularly give editorials about various development programmes/issues.

In the ultimate analysis the challenge of increasing population explosion would be met only if it is understood in the proper perspective, particularly by the political leadership. It is essential that the leadership of all the political parties at the national and state level exhibits a firm commitment towards the success of family planning programme. The programme also needs to be linked with sustainable development, environment, empowerment of women and social and gender equity.

ACKNOWLEDGEMENTS

The special issue of *Voices* (Vol. III, No. 2) 1995, *Reclaiming our Bodies* was particularly helpful in building our understanding on Reproductive Health and other connected issues.

REFERENCES

Approach Paper to the Ninth Five Year Plan (1997-2002). Government of India, Planning Commission.

Bose, Ashish (1988). *From Population to People*. BR Publishing Corporation, New Delhi.

Dreze Jean and Amartya Sen (1996). *India : Economic Development and Social Opportunity*. Oxford University Press, New Delhi.

India—1999.

India Human Development Report (1999). Oxford University Press, New Delhi.

Karnik, Kiran (1993). Communicaton Technology and Population in (ed.) Vasant Gowariker, *The Inevitable Billion*. National Book Trust, New Delhi.

Padmanabhan, B.S. (1999). Meeting the Challenge of Health, *Yojana* (42.1); Republic Day Special Issue.

State of India's Health (1992). Voluntary Health Association of India, New Delhi.

Sainath, P. (1996). *Everybody Loves a Good Drought, Stories from India's Poorest Districts*, Penguin Books (India), New Delhi.

Trakroo, P. L. and Gita Bamezai (1996). A Paradigm Shift in Communication Strategies for Health and Family Welfare Programmes in *Media Asia* 23 (3), AMIC, Singapore.

NOTE

The research study, Health and Nutrition Issues in Print Media— A Study of Some National Dailies, was conducted by Saroj Dahiya as a part of her Post-Graduate Diploma Course in Agricultural Journalism, 1999, at Haryana Agricultural University. The study deals with two major aspects : content analysis of health and nutrition news/issues, and readership behaviour of respondents regarding these issues. Five selected English newspapers; four published from New Delhi and one from Chandigarh were studied for a period of one month, 1-30 June 1999. Food and nutrition issues published in the selected newspapers for the above period comprised the sample of study.

7

Human Rights—The Challenge Ahead

Just as the world enters the new millennium, it is time to take stock of our position and progress in the domain of human rights—the most comprehensive issue encompassing almost every aspect of civil society. Before we undertake a serious study of the subject let us be clear about the term human rights. Human rights, as the term most commonly used are the rights which every human being is entitled to enjoy and to have protected. The underlying idea of such rights, which are fundamental to human dignity—is that these rights be respected in the treatment of all men, women and children. These rights exist in some form in all cultures and societies. Human rights have been legally granted to the citizens of countries all over the world. These in general terms pertain to a decent life, protection from ill health and unemployment, freedom of expression, right to education and many other rights. The urge to freedom was enshrined first in the American Declaration of Independence, 1776; and the French Declaration of Rights of Man and the Citizen and the American Bill of Rights were among the first historic initiatives to include human rights.

The contemporary international statement of these rights is the Universal Declaration of Human Rights which was adopted on 10 December 1948. The Declaration proclaims economic, social and cultural rights in addition to political and civil rights and freedom for the people of the world. These rights are considered the foundation of freedom, peace and justice in the world. Through this Declaration, the United Nations reaffirmed its faith in the worth of human beings and in the equal rights for men and women, and expressed determination to promote social progress and better standards of living for the large majority of the people.

Today human rights include right to development. Achieving development is no longer what the state may opt to "do". It is now the primary responsibility of the government to create national and international conditions favourable to the realization of the right to development. The Declaration on the right to development, which was adopted by the general assembly of the United Nations on 4 December 1986 is particularly significant for its importance to the developing countries. The Declaration states that the human person is the central subject of development and should be the active participant and beneficiary of the right to development. Article 8 in particular says

> The States should undertake, at the national level, all necessary measures for the realization of the right to development and shall ensure, *inter alia*, equality of opportunity for all in their access to basic resources, education, health services, food , housing, employment and the fair distribution of income. Effective measures should be undertaken to ensure that women have an active role in the development process.

The text of the Declaration is reproduced as Annexure at the end of the chapter, (pp. 159-165).

Promotion and protection of human rights in a plural society under a democratic framework require sustained efforts of the government and non-government organizations at different levels. An independent judiciary and vigilant media are essential institutions to safeguard people's rights.

Apart from the right to development, an other basic,

and equally significant entitlement to human survival is right to communicate. Some governments, notably the United States, have included communication rights as basic rights for their citizens. The Universal Declaration of Human Rights under Article 19 states : Every one has the right to freedom of opinion and expression; this right includes freedom to hold opinions without interference and to seek, receive and impart information and ideas through any media and regardless of frontiers. As a result the right to information and communication is receiving greater attention in the contemporary affairs.

The founding fathers of the Indian constitution attached great importance to the freedom of speech and expression, and the freedom of the Press. It has been accorded a high place in the—judgements of the apex court. Article 19(1)(a) of the Indian Constitution which embodies the freedom of Press also embraces a variety of rights. The right guaranteed is not merely the individual right of the proprietor of the newspaper, or the editor or the journalist, it includes within its compass the collective right of the community; the right of citizens to read and to be informed, to impart and receive information. In essence, it is the right of people to know. There has been a vigorous movement in several parts of the country regarding people's right to information about matters that affect them. Right to information provides a peaceful, legal procedure to expose and curb corruption. It strengthens village democracy and gives the poor and the deprived a voice. The present government, as well as the earlier ones, has acknowledged people's right to information which by all means is a vital step for good governance.

The Human Rights are universally accepted; however, a successful mechanism to enforce them is yet to be developed. The United Nations and other international organizations; several well known non-governmental organizations including Amnesty International; in India the People's Union of Civil Liberties and the media; have been spearheading a movement to create greater awareness about these rights; yet much remains to be done in this vast undone area. The media have a definite role to play in publicising these rights which is one of the most effective ways of implementation. The media must give prominent publicity to the human rights violations. Specific cases of inaction in enforcing these rights need to be highlighted. A close coordination between media and NGOs, public service and social workers and lawyers would go a long way in activating the human rights movement in the country.

That there have been large scale violations of human rights in the country—the brutality by the police force being one of the most serious one—is a recurrent theme of media reports. Two of the ghastly incidents of violence at the hands of law enforcing authorities in Tamil Nadu alone—the brutal police violence which led to the massacre of innocent men and women, primarily at Manjolai tea estate workers in Tirunelveli in July, and the riots by the inmates of Chennai Central Prison in protest against the brutalities inflicted on the prisoners by the jail staff in November, clearly show that there is hardly any regard for the human rights of the man in the street, prisoners, children or women. The *Frontline* in its issue of 24 September and the *Times of India* in its special report on 28 November, both in 1999 spell out in detail the gross violation of human rights in Tamil Nadu. In the Tirunelveli incident several non-governmental organisations and social action groups, the important being All India Democratic Women's Association, the People's Union of Civil Liberties and the Writers and Thinkers Forum for Social Harmony established fact finding teams and held public inquest. Several other groups—Human Rights Education and Protection Council, National Campaign for Dalit Human Rights and Human Rights Foundation were associated with the public inquest. The interview report of the public inquest said, "*Prima facie* evidence indicates that the police were brutal and callous in dispersing the crowds; the crowd was surrounded by the police on three sides and the only way the people could escape from the lathi charge was by jumping into the river." Could there have been an example of use of more brutal force by a law enforcing agency.

Regarding the use of prisons as correctional centres rather than torture cells, Kiran Bedi, the Magasaysay award winner, in the special report of the *Times of India* says : If prisons are not to be human warehouses but meaningful correctional centres, then they have to take charge, not merely keep charge. Prison managers must see to it that inmates use their time to re-engineer their minds—they must also provide the tools which facilitate individual recovery, whether direct or indirect, visible or invisible, conscious or subtle. Recovery should be holistic—an enabling environment must be skilfully crafted and sustained by prison managers and not imposed or introduced by inmates.

That there has been an upsurge of awareness about human rights after the imposition of Emergency by Indira Gandhi in 1975 cannot be denied. The Emergency alerted the people of India to the importance of human rights. Since the fight for civil liberties had been, from the beginning, an integral part of the Indian freedom movement, a large number of political workers, lawyers and public spirited persons stood up against the abridgement of rights of citizens during the Emergency. The Preamble to the Constitution, Fundamental Rights and Directive Principles, which together have been described as forming the Core of the Constitution reflect the basic principles of the Universal Declaration of Human Rights.

The rights include right to equality, freedom of speech, protection of life and personal liberty, protection against arrest and detention in certain cases, freedom to manage religious affairs, prohibition of traffic in human beings and forced labour, rights of minorities to establish and administer educational institutions, etc.

TABLE 6

Different Articles of Universal Declaration of Human Rights and the Indian Constitution

S. No. of Article	Universal Declaration of Human Rights	Article No.	Indian Constitution
1	2	3	4
1.	No discrimination on the ground of race, colour, sex, language, religion, birth	15	The State shall not discriminate race, colour, sex language, religion, birth, against any citizen on grounds only of religion, race, caste, sex, place of birth or any of them.
2.	Right to life	21	No person shall be deprived of his life or personal liberty except according to procedure established by law.
3.	Arbitrary arrest and detention	22	1. No person who is arrested shall be detained in custody without being informed, as soon as may be, of the grounds for such arrest nor shall he be denied the right to consult, and to be defended by, a legal practitioner of his choice. 2. Every person who is arrested and detained in custody shall be produced before the nearest magistrate within a period of twenty-four hours of such arrest excluding the time necessary for the journey from the place of arrest to the court of the magistrate and no such person shall be detained in custody beyond the said period without the authority of a magistrate.
4.	Right to religion	25	All persons are equally entitled to freedom of conscience and free profession, practice and propagation of religion.
5.	Freedom of thought and conscience	25(1)	All persons are equally entitled to freedom of conscience and the right freely to profess, practise and propagate religion.

Table 6 : contd.

1	2	3	4
6.	Freedom of information and expression	19(a)	All citizens shall have the right to speech and expression.
7.	Peaceful assembly and association	19(b)	All citizens shall have the right to assemble peaceably and without arms.
		19(c)	To form associations or unions.
8.	Right to education	45	The State shall endeavour to provide, within a period of ten years from the commencement of this Constitution, for free compulsory education for all children until they complete the age of fourteen years.

The Indian Constitution has been considered to be socio-economic instrument with a revolutionary thrust. The eminent crusaders for civil rights, Justice V. R. Krishna Iyer says : Indeed we can never forget that the people of India as a whole, not the elite nor the upper strata nor indeed the power brokers, but all the people are the title holders under the Constitution. The Fundamental Rights guaranteed under Part-III of the Constitution of India including the Right to Freedom of Speech and Expression and other rights under Article 19 cannot be appreciated and fully enjoyed unless a citizen is educated and is conscious of his individualistic dignity.

The role and contribution of judiciary in upholding public interest litigation and recognising the *locus standi* for social action groups and affirmative action has added a new dimension to the ongoing struggle for safeguarding the human rights.

Another voluntary organisation, *Common Cause* set up in 1980, and led by well known public service activist H. D. Shourie, has been taking up numerous cases of wrong doing to the pensioners by various government departments. Shourie who has been associated with drafting the Right to Information Bill, which the government proposes to introduce in the parliament during February 2000 says : Now a stage has come when people are spontaneously demanding more accountability and transparency from their government because this shroud of secrecy has bred and continues to breed corruption. And we have to make very serious, concerted efforts to rectify things. The consistent and dogged struggle of Shourie in the Supreme Court to get the pensioners their right, particularly the widows of pensioners and pension commutation, is another instance that fight for the protection of human rights needs a dogged and sustained will and determination.

Civil Society Organisations

A multitude of players outside of the government sector—grass-root organisations, trade unions, universities. non-profit foundations, user groups and non-governmental organisations influence public performance. Among the things they can hold local governments and civic bodies accountable. Such groups known—collectively as "civil society", can also aid local administration in search for more responsive and effective governance. In India, and more so at the international level, the increasing role of non-governmental organisations, voluntary bodies and other organs of the civil society in advocacy and policy formulation has introduced a new element in democratic governance. In the contemporary society policy formulation is not left to governments alone. In the Foreword to a book *Public Policy, Analysis and Design*, the eminent Indian diplomat, economist and educational administrator, A. M. Khusro says : Policy need not be made by governments only, but in this country policy has been made almost wholly by governments. It may be because other segments and sectors—the commercial sector and the social sector, have been weak and are in the throes of a slow developmental process, they will acquire a degree of resilience and a policy making capability later. But to begin with they were weak and therefore, it fell to the lot of central and state governments to make policies and programmes during the last 40 years. There are NGOs like Policy Initiatives or Policy Alternatives, etc. and there are associations of industry and trade. Many people in the private sector of industry and trade, the cooperative sector. the NGO sector, the social sector and intellectual sector, are beginning to think of many policy areas and it is certain that their role will increase with time.

The special issue of *Development Dialogue*, published by Dag Hammarskjold Foundation devotes one paper to the responsibilities of civil society organisations. In the systems analysis, the paper makes fascinating study : In eighties the First System comprised princes (the politicians and the governments); while the second position fell to merchants (now transnational enterprises). Today the reality is otherwise. In several countries including USA, UK, Canada, Australia and Japan, the merchants dictate to the princes. Globalisation has become a corporate *mantra* mouthed by politicians. It is widely known that US corporations do not act for the benefit of US economy. The Second System is under attack from CSOs, which constitute the Third System. Increasingly the disenchanted sectors of civil society are asking—Why governments who cannot deliver services should be permitted to set policies. In any future dispensation CSOs will be forced to take a more aggressive policy role.

We may recall that it is because of the sustained hard work put in by organisations like NBA that today even the World Bank has agreed to revisit the claims of big dams and irrigation projects. It is only because of the critical scrutiny of the CSOs that the role of international conferences like the Earth Summit and the Beijing Conference is being evaluated for concrete results.

Erosion of rights is one area where challenge to human dignity is the greatest. CSOs are increasingly looking to constitutional and legal remedies for safeguarding human rights mechanisms to counter the force of World Trade Organisation (see the devastating effect with which the recent WTO conference in US was confronted by NGOs and VOs). The invocation of human rights (which would include freedom of expression, of the press, right to development, political opinion and education) draws together a broad spectrum of civil society and holds real promise of success.

We have seen how several CSOs have made effective intervention regarding Freedom of Information Act. Another such no profit trust voices has been working as a communication resource and advocacy group. The Bangalore-based media NGO, Madhyam Communications has been spearheading a movement to examine issues relating to democratisation in media, the right to communicate and access to information and communication technologies particularly by the economically and socially deprived. Its journal provides a forum to a vast cross-section of the media academics and scholars, working in the voluntary and social sectors and all others interested in working for change in the society and protect human rights.

There is certainly greater need for many more voluntary bodies and human rights groups to work in close coordination and take up cases of the affected persons with the courts. After independence, and particularly in the wake of JP movement and the movement of parliamentary opposition parties against the Emergency several prominent organisations including citizens for Democracy (1973) and People's Union for Civil Liberties and Democratic Rights (1976) emerged.

Writing on human rights action groups in India, An Historical Outline, Sitharamam Kakarala says : The internal emergency proclaimed in June 1975 played an important role in bringing issues of human rights to the common agenda of mass movements and political parties with different ideologies. In a way, human rights because a rallying point for united action. The emergency also helped the middle classes in India to see civil liberties and only human rights as more democratic issues than issues only of left wing political parties and movements. It also highlighted the need for conscious public scrutiny of governmental institutions, however, legitimately they might have been constituted. It also helped to dissociate human rights action from political ideologies and parties of all varieties, *Voices for Change*, II(3).

One of the noteworthy instances of media taking the issue of human rights is the special issue of *Voices*

(December 1998), brought out by the Madhyam Communications—a non-profit trust working for positive changes in the Indian society which will lead to a more just and egalitarian social order. The Foreword to the above issue says : In a country where at least a third of the people have to wage a daily and seemingly unending struggle for basic needs like food, water and shelter, as well as essential services such as health care, education and mechanisms for social security, and where a significant number continues to face humiliation, discrimination and oppression on account of sex, caste and/or ethnic origins, the struggle for human rights has perforce to go beyond highlighting specific atrocities committed by agencies of the state or any body else.

The role of media in creating awareness about human rights violations goes beyond reporting such incidents. Media provides an enabling environment, it creates ideology; it also helps make people's mind and develop attitude. Media is a powerful instrument; therefore it is important that the media potential in strengthening human rights movements be fully utilised. Media coverage of human rights issues has not been very satisfactory, it has at best been sporadic and event-oriented. The study of leading newspapers conducted by A. K. Singh about development journalism in India shows that human rights coverage was still one of the most neglected subjects. The reports of international organisations were given greater importance in newspapers. It was also observed that such reports were often big sources of information for writing editorials, news and articles on human rights violation. The child labour issue was another important item for news, views and articles in the newspapers. The movement of different organisations against child labour is one of the important reasons for giving attention to this issue. Media indeed has to go a long way in making human rights issues as a regular subject for reporting, analysing and interpreting.

Interestingly, it is sometimes contended that the frequent reporting of human rights violations on TV coarsens our sensibilities towards the sufferings of the subject community. Delivering the Dag Hammarskjold Lecture on 1 October 1998 in Uppsala. the UN High Commissioner for Human Rights, Mary Robinson said As we mark the 50th Anniversary of the Universal Declaration of Human Rights and engage in the stocktaking review after five years of the Vienna Declaration and Programme of Action, it is deeply disturbing to recall that every day, hundreds of millions of people experience some serious violations of their human rights. Increasingly, as we watch their suffering on TV, we seem to have a capacity to distance ourselves : to go and make some coffee, take a phone call. There is a worrying correlation between the immediacy of our knowledge and our capacity to distance ourselves. Many of those who suffer are children, women, old people, people with disabilities, minorities, migrants and indigenous peoples.

Robinson also said : Independent national human rights commissions can by virtue of their accessibility, transform the rhetoric of international instruments into practical reality and provide redress for millions of people. They can do this in a manner which is consistent with the international standards prescribed in international treaties, while accommodating constitutional peculiarities and the extraordinarily disparate challenges posed by local conditions and cultures—thus respecting ethnic, cultural, religious and linguistic diversity but not allowing it to compromise the universality of human rights.

The National Human Rights Commission in India was constituted in October 1993, under the Human Rights Ordinance of September 1993. The commission, a fully autonomous body, is headed by the Chairperson who has been the Chief Justice of the Supreme Court. and one member among others, who is, or has been a judge of the Supreme Court. The Commission is empowered to look into violation of human rights and take suitable action. The initiative taken by the Commission recently in directing the Orissa government to take immediate steps for proper distribution of relief measures among the people affected by super-cyclone has given the common man some hope that he has a forum where public grievances would be taken care at the humanitarian level.

REFERENCES

Human Rights. the New Consensus (1994). Regency Press in association with United Nations High Commissioner for Refugees. New York.

Iyer. V. R. Krishna. The Law's Zigzag Course in. *India at 50. Bliss of Hope and Burden of Reality* (eds) V. N. Narayanan and Jyoti Sabharwal. Sterling Publishers Private Limited, New Delhi.

Singh. A. K. (1999). Development Journalism in India (A Study of Leading Newspapers). Unpublished Ph. D. Thesis. Banaras Hindu University. Varanasi.

Voices—for change Vol 2. No. 3. Understanding Human Rights (1998). Benson Town. Bangalore.

Annexure

DECLARATION ON THE RIGHT TO DEVELOPMENT

A landmark development in the formulation and recognition of new human rights is the Declaration on the Right to Development which was adopted by the General Assembly of the United Nations on 4 December 1986. This Declaration is particularly significant for its importance to the developing countries, even though the necessary means for enforcing it are lacking. The text of this Declaration is reproduced below

The General Assembly

Bearing in mind the purposes and principles of the Charter of the United Nations relating to the achievement of international co-operation in solving international problems of economic, social, cultural or humanitarian nature, and in promoting and encouraging respect for human rights and fundamental freedoms for all without distinction as to race, sex, language or religion.

Recognizing the development is a comprehensive economic, social, cultural and political process, which aims at the constant improvement of the well-being of the entire population and of all individuals on the basis of their active, free and meaningful participation in development and in the fair distribution of benefits resulting therefrom.

Considering that under the provisions of the Universal Declaration of Human Rights everyone is entitled to a social and international order in which the rights and freedoms set forth in the Declaration can be fully realized.

Recalling the provisions of the International Covenant of Economic, Social and Cultural Rights and of the International Covenant on Civil and Political Rights.

Recalling further the relevant agreements, conventions, resolutions, recommendations and other instruments of the United Nations and its specialized agencies concerning the integral development of the human being, economic and social progress and development of all peoples, including those instruments concerning decolonization, the prevention of discrimination, respect for and observance of human rights and fundamental freedoms, the maintenance of international peace and security and the further promotion of friendly relations and cooperation among States in accordance with the Charter.

Recalling the right of peoples to self-determination, by virtue of which they have the right freely to determine their political status and to pursue their economic, social and cultural development.

Recalling also the right of peoples to exercise, subject to the relevant provisions of both International Covenants of Human Rights, full and complete sovereignty over all their natural wealth and resources.

Mindful of the obligation of States under the Charter to promote universal respect for and observance of human rights and fundamental freedoms for all without distinction of any kind such as race, colour, sex, language, religion, political or other opinion, national or social origin, property, birth or other status.

Considering that the elimination of the massive and flagrant violations of the human rights of the peoples and individuals affected by situations such as those resulting from colonialism, neo-colonialism, apartheid, all forms of racism and racial discrimination, foreign domination and occupation, aggression and threats against national sovereignty, national unity and territorial integrity and threats of war would contribute to the establishment of circumstances propitious to the development of a great part of mankind.

Concerned at the existence of serious obstacles to development, as well as to the complete fulfilment of human beings and of peoples, constituted, *inter alia*, by the denial of civil, political, economic, social and cultural rights, and considering that all human rights and fundamental freedoms are indivisible and interdependent and that, in order to promote development, equal attention, and urgent consideration should be given to the implementation, promotion and protection of civil, political, economic, social and cultural rights and that accordingly, the promotion of, respect for and enjoyment of certain human rights and fundamental freedoms cannot justify the denial of other human rights and fundamental freedoms.

Considering that international peace and security are essential elements for the realization of the right to development.

Reaffirming that there is a close relationship between disarmament and development and that progress in the field of disarmament would considerably promote progress in the field of development and that resources released through disarmament measures should be devoted to the economic and social development and well-being of all peoples and, in particular, those of the developing countries.

Recognizing that the human person is the central subject of the development process and that development policy should therefore make the human being the main participant and beneficiary of development.

Recognizing that the creation of conditions favourable to the development of peoples and individuals is the primary responsibility of their States.

Aware that efforts at the international level to promote and protect human rights should be accompanied by efforts to establish a new international economic order.

Confirming that the right to development is an inalienable human right and that equality of opportunity for development is a prerogative both of nations and of individuals who make up nations.

Proclaims the following Declaration on the Right to Development

Article 1

1. The right to development is an inalienable human right by virtue of which every human person and all peoples are entitled to participate in, contribute to and enjoy economic, social, cultural and political development, in which all human rights and fundamental freedoms

can be fully realized.

2. The human right to development also implies the full realization of the right of peoples to self-determination, which includes, subject to the relevant provisions of both International Covenants on Human Rights, the exercise of their inalienable right to full sovereignty over all their natural wealth and resources.

Article 2

1. The human person is the central subject of development and should be the active participant and beneficiary of the right to development.
2. All human beings have a responsibility for development, individually and collectively, taking into account the need for full respect for their human rights and fundamental freedoms as well as their duties to the community, which alone can ensure the free and complete fulfilment of the human being and they should therefore promote and protect an appropriate political, social and economic order for development.
3. States have the right and the duty to formulate appropriate national development policies that aim at constant improvement of the well-being of the entire population and of all individuals, on the basis of their active, free and meaningful participation in development and in the fair distribution of the benefits resulting therefrom.

Article 3

1. States have the primary responsibility for the creation of national and international conditions favourable to the realization of the right to development.
2. The realization of the right to development requires full respect for the principles of international law concerning friendly relations and cooperation among States in accordance with the Charter of the United Nations.
3. States have the duty to cooperate with each other in

ensuring development and eliminating obstacles to development. States should realize their rights and fulfil their duties in such a manner as to promote a new international economic order based on sovereign equality, interdependence, mutual interest and cooperation among all States, as well as to encourage the observance and realization of human rights.

Article 4

1. States have the duty to take steps, individually and collectively, to formulate international development policies with a view to facilitating the full realization of the right to development.
2. Sustained action is required to promote more rapid development of developing countries. As a complement to the efforts of developing countries, effective international cooperation is essential in providing these countries with appropriate means and facilities to foster their comprehensive development.

Article 5

States shall take resolute steps to eliminate the massive and flagrant violations of the human rights of peoples and human beings affected by situations such as those resulting from apartheid, all forms of racism and racial discrimination, colonialism, foreign domination and occupation, aggression, foreign interference and threats against national sovereignty, national unity and territorial integrity, threats of war and refusal to recognize the fundamental right of peoples to self-determination.

Article 6

1. All States should cooperate with a view to promoting, encouraging and strengthening universal respect for an observance of all human rights and fundamental freedoms for all without any distinction as to race, sex, language or religion.

2. All human rights and fundamental freedoms are indivisible and interdependent; equal attention and urgent consideration should be given to the implementation, promotion and protection of civil, political, economic, social and cultural rights.
3. States should take steps to eliminate obstacles to development resulting from failure to observe civil and political rights, as well as economic, social and cultural rights.

Article 7

All States should promote the establishment, maintenance and strengthening of international peace and security and, to that end, should do their utmost to achieve general and complete disarmament under effective international control, as well as to ensure that the resources released by effective disarmament measures are used for comprehensive development, in particular that of the developing countries.

Article 8

1. States should undertake, at the national level, all necessary measures for the realization of the right to development and shall ensure, *inter alia*, equality of opportunity for all in their access to basic resources, education, health services, food, housing, employment and the fair distribution of income. Effective measures should be undertaken to ensure that women have an active role in the development process. Appropriate economic and social reforms should be carried out with a view to eradicating all social injustices.
2. States should encourage popular participation in all spheres as an important factor in development and in the full realization of all human rights.

Article 9

1. All the aspects of the right to development set forth in

the present Declaration are indivisible and interdependent and each of them should be considered in the context of the whole.

2. Nothing in the present Declaration shall be construed as being contrary to the purposes and principles of the United Nations, or as implying that any State, group or person has a right to engage in any activity or to perform any act aimed at the violation of the rights set forth in the Universal Declaration of Human Rights and in the International Covenants on Human Rights.

Article 10

Steps should be taken to ensure the full exercise and progressive enhancement of the right to development, including formulation, adoption and implementation of policy, legislative and other measures at the national and international levels.

8

Environmental Protection—The Battle for Survival

The history of life on earth has been a history of interaction between living things and their surroundings. To a large extent, the physical form and the habits of the earth vegetation and the animal life have been moulded by the environment. Considering the whole span of earthly time, the opposite effect, in which Life actually modifies its surroundings has been relatively slight. Only within ..... the present century has one species-man-acquired significant power to alter the nature of his world.

Alongwith the possibility of....... nuclear war, the central problem of our age has therefore become the contamination of man's total environment with substances of incredible potential for harm.

Rachel Carson

Silent Spring, 1962

An early warning of mankind's suicidal destruction of the natural world—*Silent Spring* was a wake up call that crystallized those concerns (increasing destructive effects of technology on the natural world).

Time—Great People of the 20th Century

Published in 1962, the *Silent Spring* became a runaway best seller and proved extremely effective in focusing on the central issue of the deadly impact of chemical pesticides. The book, a wake up call firmly placed the issue of conserving natural resources on century's agenda and in a way pioneered the environmental movement. It became an important means of creating awareness about environmental protection. As a mass medium the book reached millions of people not only in US but in other countries as well. Works such as *Silent Spring* help shape the environmental protection and take up causes which have already become central concerns for the 21st century.

Let us see what the *one species* (man) has done since the wake up call given in the *Silent Spring* in 1962? Two examples :

Between 1975 and 1995, when the Indian economy doubled, *industrial pollution levels went up four times and vehicular eight times* and we could see what single rupee of economic growth could do. It is already impossible to breathe in most Indian cities and towns and we are just beginning to industrialise, just beginning to motorise.

Anil Aggarwal, Environment—The Battle Ahead
A Future Past the Present—Hindustan Times 2000

"Save our Skies—Be Ozone Friendly", the theme of the September 16 International Day for the Protection of the Ozone Layer, tried to sharpen the focus and raise global awareness on the importance of preserving the Ozone Layer by taking industrial action to reduce and eliminate impacts on the stratospheric ozone layer caused by the products that you buy, the appliances and equipment that your household or business uses, or the manufacturing process used by your company (The rich countries could buy the right to pollute).

Times of India, 13-9-1999

The battle ranging to protect environment has truly assumed epic proportions—the battle is no less to protect over very survival : our skies, the air we breathe, the water we drink and the food we eat. This is the major challenge that the mankind faces in the 21st century. All our strategies for development would be negated if we do not take up in the right earnest the challenge of environmental protection.

In India the people-led movements have gone a long way in effectively opposing the ecologically harmful policies of the government. One of the foremost of such movements *chipko* movement, which began in April 1973, was essentially an initiative for forest protection and regeneration. The movement of hill people of Uttar Pradesh protested against the exploitation of forest resources by contractor from outside. This movement also inspired Appiko movement in the Southern parts of India in which people were actively involved in stopping illegal over felling of forests.

The first major breakthrough achieved by environmentalists was their success in preventing the construction of a hydro-electric plant in Silent Valley, Kerala in 1982. Several important and basic issues were involved in the controversy—Economy Vs Ecology; as well as the differing perceptions of two categories of thinking—"developmentalist" vs "environmentalist'. The environmentalists wanted to prevent the Kunthi river in Palaghat district from being damed to create a reservoir for the generation of electricity. The environmental groups were supported by the Kerala Sastra Sahitya Parishad; whereas the developmentalists were supported by the state government, all the political parties and some scientists who found no justification for the environmentalists to go that far to stop a developmental project. The decision on whether to build a dam was held in abeyance for eight years and finally dropped thus saving a precious heritage of botanical and genetic diversity almost unique in nature. The struggle by the KSSP and other environmental groups succeeded in pointing out that it was possible to develop without destroying the natural resources which are essential for the very survival of mankind. The ecological conflicts, including construction of large hydro-electrical projects and big dams, with support from international organizations including World Bank, have added an entirely new dimension to the model of development we are pursuing. The observations of Vandana Shiva in her book :

Ecology and the Politics of Survival—Conflicts over Natural Resources in India, are noteworthy : Since large water projects for power and irrigation are capital-intensive, they have usually been financed by international aid. World Bank loans have made a significant contribution to the construction of large dams and canal systems in post-independent India. The role of the World Bank and other sources of multi-lateral and bilateral development aid in the construction of gigantic projects with heavy social and ecological costs is generating a new level of conflict between the interests of international agencies and local communities. A new era of ecological politics is unfolding in which people affected by ecologically destructive projects are trying to make international financial institutes accountable for their landing practices.

In a way the 1980s were a watershed decade for the environmental projects movements to flourish, environmental protests and awareness gained ground and environmental issues came upon the agenda of policy makers and planners. This period also saw massive protest movements in different parts of the country against steps which degraded environment and eroded the quality of life. One of the most widespread agitations which culminated in a massive rally at Harsud, Madhya Pradesh in October 1989 was the protest against Narmada Valley Project.

At this rally for the first time different environmental groups from all over the country came together. The ecological viability of building large dams was questioned by environmentalists and social activists. The long term effects of such dams include threat of large scale submersion of forest and agricultural lands, soil salinity and waterlogging are affecting adversely best food growing lands and dense forests. While tangible benefits are debatable, human problems like relocations and rehabilitations, threat to wild life and other associated harmful results has induced rethinking about the utility of big dams at the World Bank level. During the decade industrial pollution and environmental negligence took on alarming proportions. Industrial plants, producing dangerous chemicals for use in pesticides and fertilizers. located near densely populated towns posed a definite hazard to the people. The leakage of deadly Methyl Iso Cyanate gas from the pesticide plant of Union Carbide (India) Limited, causing worst industrial disaster resulting in the death of 4000 persons and leaving 2,00,000 injured culminated in Bhopal Gas Tragedy. The Bhopal Disaster triggered the Environmental Protection Act in 1986. Such mishaps occur frequently because of the irresponsibility of the industry and the uncaring attitude of the government. The Union Carbide case is quoted because it was the extreme example of air pollution, but cumulatively thousands of undertakings which emit toxic fumes cause far more damage to human health than a single Union Carbide.

It is now being increasingly realised that demography is not merely a question of numbers of people. When the carrying capacity of planet Earth reaches the point of exhaustion, as is the case with countries like India, China and Indonesia, an environmental disaster is waiting to happen any moment. Essentially we need resources which provide medical care for 1 billion people in the country; and it is the earth's natural resources which provide for meeting all the above needs. As these resources deplete and the population keeps growing, the rate of depletion also increases because the dwindling resources are required to cater to more people. In this context we must take note of the process of invisible destruction of resources which constitute the basis for the survival of millions of people. Vandana Shiva says : The illusions of the contemporary take-off stage in countries like India and the vision of a flight to the twenty-first century are made possible through a similar process of the invisible destruction of the base for survival of millions of marginal people. The opposition of ecology movements to resource destructive development and growth is rooted in the recognition that the creation of resources for growth is achieved through the destruction of resources for the survival of people. Ever expanding consumption puts strains on environment-emissions and was that pollute the earth and destroy ecosystems. and growing depletion and degradation of renewable resources that undermines livelihoods. Runaway growth in consumption in the past 50 years is putting strain on the environment never before seen.

The efforts of NGO's, environmental groups, institutions like Centre for Science and Environment (CSE) and individuals : Chandi Prasad Bhat, Sunderlal Bahuguna, Medha Patakar, Anil Agarwal. Vandana Shiva and journalists like Bharat Dogra have gone a long way in creating awareness about different aspects of environmental problems. The journal brought out by CSE, Down to Earth, has significantly contributed in making available research based articles and knowledge to the students, academic community, planners and policy makers. The awareness of and awakening to the seriousness of the problem—which challenge the very survival of the people and people's involvement would help environmental issues being on the agenda of political parties and ultimately the nation. In not too distant a future the movement for environmental protection may emerge as people's movement nationwide. What is needed is : consolidation of the movement on the pattern of *Greens* in *Europe*, whereby entering the political arena they are fighting elections on an ecological platform they have also been able to enlist the popular support of the political parties. The greens succeeded in converting even Margaret Thatcher to the cause of conservation.

Another aspect to the consolidation of environmental movement is the judicial intervention at the highest level by the Supreme Court. The check on the pollution caused by the vehicular traffic in a capital city like Delhi could not have been imposed but for the repeated and forceful intervention of the Supreme Court. The government system has all but collapsed; and the Government of Delhi, instead of enthusiastically implementing the decisions of the Supreme Court (which the government, if it were sensitive to the problems of pollution should have taken the initiative by itself) comes up with some alibi for not been able to carry out the orders of the highest court of the land. Public interest litigation (PIL), launched by social activists to protect green belt in towns from encroachment at the hands of Municipal Corporations and builders, seeking the intervention of the courts on different issues—right from protecting the Taj to introduction of leadfree petrol, and other environment-related problems. The fact of the matter is that the courts of the country have come to the rescue of environmentalists where the local administration or the government failed to take effective measures to enforce legal provisions. Apart from the pioneers in environmental movements, journalists, writers and researchers, several lawyers and judges have contributed magnificently in this battle against degradation of environment.

No discussion on environmental protection could be considered to be complete without reference to the report of the World Commission on Environment and Development, *Our Common Future*, which gave a new direction in which the developmental efforts need to be directed. The report pointed out that 'content of economic growth would have to change' and that 'even consumption of material goods should be ranked according to a scale of sustainability'. Another important observation in the report pertains to the holistic nature of environment. The environment does not exist as sphere separate from human actions, ambitions and needs and attempts to defend it in isolation from human concerns has given the very word "environment", a connotation of naivety in some political circles.

The report recognized the relationship of environmental and developmental concerns and proposed a number of long range steps for changing conditions and practices which threaten human survival

> *Many critical survival issues are related to uneven development, poverty, and pollution growth. They all place unprecedented pressures on the planet's lands, waters, forests, and other natural resources, not least in the developing countries. The downward spiral of poverty and environmental degradation is a waste of opportunities and of resources. In particular, it is a waste of human resources. These links between poverty,*

inequality and environmental degradation formed a major theme in our analysis and recommendations. What is needed now is a new era of economic growth—growth that is forceful and at the same time socially and environmentally sustainable.

The World Development Report* 1999/2000, *Entering the 21st Century*, defines Sustainable Development as Any sustainable development agenda must be concerned with intergenerational equity—that is that future generations have the same capability to develop as the present generation. A development path is sustainable only if it ensures that the stock of overall capital assets remains constant or increases over time. These assets include manufactured capital (such as machines and roads), human capital (knowledge and skills), social capital (relationships and institutions), and environmental capital (forests and coral reefs). This environment matters not just because of its effect on psychic and non-economic welfare but also because of its impact on production over the long term.

Environmental sustainability is also connected with intergenerational equity. While the wealthy consume more resources overall, the poor tend to rely more heavily on the direct exploitation of natural resources than the rich. If they have no access to non-environmental resources and so have limited capacity to adopt they may have no choice but to engage in unsustainable uses of environmental resources.

**Box 8, p-28*

With the awareness creeping in at the national and international levels—thanks to the consistent efforts made for more than two past decades by the civil society organisations, inter-governmental and international organisations, a major rethinking of our environmental strategies and action plans is starting to take shape with a shift in focus towards strategic outcomes : the big challenge will be for all stake holders to agree on which outcomes matter most, offering hope and opportunity not only for this generation, but for future generations to come. This essentially is sustainable development all about.

The over use of natural resources result in not only in resource depletion and ecological degradation that threaten the livelihood of poor but also result in high environmental health risks, manifested by high infant and child mortality and high morbidity specially among the rural poor. The principal causes are all environment related—poor quality of drinking water supply and lack of sanitation, indoor and outdoor air pollution and toxic and hazardous agro industrial waste disposal and discharges.

An interesting aspect, which, makes refreshing break from the strait-jacket treatment that environment as a discipline has been subject to, is the World Bank's new strategy in putting particular emphasis on understanding the contribution of environmental activities to poverty is different to define. It is cross sectoral and multi disciplinary and can mean different things to different people. Traditionally indicators of income and consumption have been used to define poverty but now the definitions broadening to include such a health, education, security and political voice. Environmental activities are linked to poverty reduction; one direct link, for instance is through the health of the poor. Many studies have shown that clean drinking water and sanitation are important for health. It has been found that the two biggest causes of death of the poor were respiratory infections and diarrheal diseases. Both are linked to environmental factors—dirty water and dirty air. Sixty per cent of all malaria deaths occur among the poorest 20 per cent of world's population. Another Bank study estimates that in the Indian state of Andhra Pradesh, the Bank could reduce the burden of disease by 17 per cent with three activities—providing clean drinking water from taps inside the house, providing private latrines and reducing indoor air pollution through clean cooking fuel. But on the chapter, Poverty and Environment, from Annual Review, Environment Matters at the World Bank, 1999.

Apart from a number of initiatives taken by international institutes, civil organisations and voluntary groups, towards upholding and strengthening the cause of environmental protection. Amartya Sen pleads for public action for the same purpose. There are many relevant fields, land reform, local democracy, women's action but also others including sound environmental policies, improved rural infrastructure, where the potential role of state is potentially quite extensive; but at the same time standard of activity in many of these fields is abysmally related to 'public action'. Thus, political parties and public activists have an important role in the emergence of particular policies. India's democratic institutions provide many potential basis of public action—including not only the electoral process but also the news media the legal system, the village panchayats, etc. but an important organisational task is involved in seizing these opportunities.

In the meanwhile some politicians like the Madhya Pradesh Chief Minister Digvijay Singh have taken initiative in certain schemes like watershed management project. In case CSOs, public action and political parties involve a broad consensus and join hands in bringing up environment protection on the national agenda, there is no reason to believe as to why our battle of survival does not become much less intractable.

REFERENCES

Anil Agarwal (2000). Environment—The Battle Ahead in A Future Past the Present. *Hindustan Times.*

Darryl D'Monte (1984). *Silent Valley : The Silence Returns. The Illustrated Weekly of India*, 15-21 April.

Dreze Jean and Amartya Sen (1995). *India : Economic Development and Social Opportunity.* Oxford University Press.

ESCAP (1988). *Reporting on the Environment—A Handbook for Journalists*, Bangkok.

Rachel Carson (1998). In : *Great People of the 20th Century, Time.*

Shiva, Vandana (1997). *Ecology and the Politics of Survival, Conflicts over Natural Resources in India.* Sage Publications, New Delhi.

World Development Report 1999/2000. *Entering the 21st Century.* The World Bank, Washington.

World Bank (1999). *Environment Matters—Annual Review.*

Bibliography

An Indian Personality for Television (1985). Report of the Working Group on Software for Doordarshan. Ministry of Information and Broadcasting, New Delhi.

Asian Mass Communication Research and Information Centre (1996). *Opening Windows—Issues in Communication*, Singapore.

Chandra, Bipan (1993). *Essays on Contemporary India.* Har-Anand Publications, New Delhi.

Dreze, Jean and Sen, Amartya (1995). *India : Economic Development and Social Opportunity.* Oxford University Press, Oxford and New Delhi.

Gowariker, Vasant (ed.) (1993). *The Inevitable Billion Plus.* National Book Trust, New Delhi.

Gupta, V. S. (1995). *Third Revolution in Indian Perspective—Contemporary Issues and Themes in Communication.* Concept Publishing Company, New Delhi.

Gupta, V. S. and Aggarwal, Vir Bala (1996). *Media Policy and Nation Building, Select Issues and Themes.* Concept Publishing Company, New Delhi.

Gupta, V. S. (1996). Media Strategies for Rural Development. *Kurukshetra* XLIV (4-5). Publications Division, New Delhi.

Gupta, V. S. and Dyal, Rajeshwar (eds.) (1996). *National Media Policy.* Concept Publishing Company, New Delhi.

This bibliography contains a list of only those sources which have been actually used in the book, and not the many others which have been consulted by the author but not specifically used. Minor references in the text, such as references to newspapers, have been omitted.

Gupta, V. S. (1999). *Communication Technology, Media Policy and National Development.* Concept Publishing Company, New Delhi.

Human Rights—The New Consensus (1994). Regency Press, Golden House, London.

Independent Commission on Population and Quality of Life (1996). *Caring for the Future.* Oxford University Press, Oxford.

India Today (1998) Vol. XXIII, No. 43. Poverty's Philosopher —Amartya Sen, New Delhi.

India 1999 (A reference Annual). Publications Division, Ministry of Information and Broadcasting, Government of India, New Delhi.

Joshi, P. C. (1986). *Communication and Nation-Building : Perspective and Policy.* Sardar Patel Memorial Lectures, Publications Division, New Delhi.

Kunczik, Michael (1992). *Development and Communication.* Friedrich-Ebert Stiftung, Bonn.

Melkote, Srinivas R. (1991). *Communication for Development in the Third World—Theory and Practice.* Sage Publications, New Delhi.

Mody, Bella (1991). *Designing Messages for Development Communication.* Sage Publications, New Delhi.

Nair, K. S. and White, S. A. (1993). *Perspectives on Development Communication.* Sage Publications, New Delhi.

Narayanan, V. N. and Sabharwal, Jyoti (1997). *India at 50, Bliss of Hope and Burden of Reality.* Sterling Publishers, New Delhi.

Phadnis, Umashanker (ed.) (1998). *Exploring the Heartland —An Agenda for the Media.* Gyan Publishing House, New Delhi.

Proceedings of the D. T. Lakdawala Memorial Symposium (1994). *Decentralised Planning and Panchayati Raj.* Concept Publishing Company, New Delhi.

Rao, U. R. (1996). *Space Technology for Sustainable Development.* Tata McGraw Hill Publishing Company, New Delhi.

Sainath, P. (1996). *Everybody Loves a Good Drought—Stories from India's poorest districts.* Penguin Books,

New Delhi.

Shiva Vandana (1991). *Ecology and the Politics of Survival—Conflicts over Natural Resources in India.* Sage Publications, New Delhi.

Shariff, Abusaleh (1999). *India : Human Development Report.* National Council of Applied Economic Research, New Delhi.

Singhal, Arvind and Rogers, Everett M. (1989). *India's Information Revolution.* Sage Publications, New Delhi.

Teheranian Majid, Hakimzadeh, Farhad and Vidale, Marcello L. (eds.) (1977). *Communication Policy for National Development.* Routledge and Kegan Paul, London.

Toffler, Alvin (1980). *The Third Wave.* William Collins, London.

UNDP (1993). *Human Development Report.* Oxford University Press, Oxford.

UNDP (1996). *Human Development Report.* Oxford University Press. Oxford.

UNESCO (1982). *Many Voices, One World.* The International Commission on the Study of Communication Problems, Paris.

UNESCO (1996). *Learning : The Treasure Within.* Paris.

UNESCO (1997). *World Information Report* 1997-98. Paris.

UNESCO (1997). *Public Service Broadcasting : The Challenge of the Twenty-first Century*, Paris.

Venkateswaran, Sandhya (1995). *Environment, Development and the Gender Gap.* Sage Publications, New Delhi.

Voices (1997). *Media Policy and Community Radio.* Bangalore.

World Bank (1996). *From Plan to Market.* Oxford University Press, Oxford.

World Bank (1999). *Knowledge for Development.* Oxford University Press, Oxford.

World Bank (2000). *Entering the 21st Century.* Oxford University Press, Oxford.

Index